FINANCIAL FOREPLAY

WHIP YOUR BUSINESS INTO SHAPE & TAKE HOME MORE CASH

RHONDALYNN KOROLAK

Cover Design by Chameleon Print Design
Cover and Author photograph: Yusuke Sato
Typeset by BookPOD

This book is available for purchase from:-
www.imagineeringnow.com www.imagineeringunlimited.com

Financia Foreplay® - Whip Your Business into Shape and Take Home More Cash / Rhondalynn Korolak

Library of Congress Control Number: 2008910915

ISBN: 9780980557817 (pbk.)

Acknowledgements

Perhaps the most significant learning of my life is this: if you want to make a new contribution, promote understanding and inspire change you have to be willing to look at what you do from a completely new perspective and take a risk. Financial Foreplay® is a marked deviation from anything that I have ever done before. It doesn't look or read anything like an accounting or finance book... and therein lies its charm and potency. The book was born out of a very simple desire to help business owners with some of their most formidable challenges – enhancing profitability and cash flow, reducing risk, knowing what to measure and focus attention on and identifying opportunities. That desire combined with the input and talent of some special people has produced a book that I am extremely excited about.

The success of this book and the overwhelming media support is largely due to the effort of some very talented people. David Brewster, who helped me to bring this material to life in way that is memorable, thought provoking and empowering. Without him, this project could have easily been "just another finance book" that no one wants to read. His vision, influence and expertise really brought the client stories to life in a way that will resonate with the millions of entrepreneurs who are struggling right now day-to-day in their businesses.

Thanks also to Clare Hallifax, my trusted editor, for her attention to detail and feedback, Sylvie and Michael Blair from Bookpod and the team at Sexyland for providing the props for our cover shoot. My deepest appreciation also goes to the many men and women from companies large and small who have allowed me to share their experiences, challenges, stories and success.

Contents

Introduction

If you are like most small business owners I work with, you went into business because you are good at what you do – graphic design, hospitality, construction, farming, retailing – and you wanted the autonomy and financial freedom of owning your own business. You were probably thinking, "as long as I am good at what I do, how hard can it be to make a decent living and support my family?" And you have probably discovered that it is harder than you thought.

You may be one of the 95% of small business owners who discover that although they work like dogs every day, they have little to show for it. You may be one of the many who find themselves isolated because they don't feel there is anyone to discuss or share their greatest fears and challenges with.

You may be feeling overwhelmed right now by any number of issues. Your workload, a shortage of customers, supplier issues, customer service challenges and the fact that there never seems to be enough time to plan ahead, to budget or review your progress. Or you may simply be wondering why you never seem to have any extra money, even though your accountant says that you are making a profit.

Which leads me to one area I'm guessing is definitely harder to grasp than you thought it would be: the management of money.

If you are like most small business owners I work with, you never dreamed that the ability to understand how money works would be very important. You thought: "That's for the accountant (or bookkeeper) to worry about. Sure, the accountant shows me a few reports from time to time, but I don't see the need to *really* understand what they mean. If there was a problem, he would tell me, wouldn't he?".

You probably don't realize that all those numbers - the financial DNA of your business - can tell you a lot more than you thought. They can tell you why you're suddenly struggling to pay the bills. They can explain why your business is not performing as well as you thought it would - or as well as you were promised it would when you bought it. They can reveal why you'll have to forego your salary - again - because there just isn't enough cash.

The financial numbers of your business are the story of your business. The numbers don't lie. They are one of the few objective indicators of how your business is performing and where the problems are. Regardless of any justifications you use to explain why your business is not performing - the economy, the shortage of 'good' staff, the competition, the rent - the numbers tell the truth and can lead you to the solution. You just need to learn HOW to use them to your advantage.

You need a bit of *Financial Foreplay®*.

In this book you will learn:

- Why cash, more than profit, is the key to success in business;
- How to find and unlock the hidden profit and cash that are trapped in your business;
- How to use the numbers in your financial statements to give you information that is useful for you - not just useful for your accountant. For instance, I'll show you how to calculate a few simple but important ratios, to understand the results and to monitor them on an ongoing basis;
- How to stop making common business mistakes that are preventing you from being as successful as you deserve to be;.
- Why too much inventory can strangle your business;
- How to manage debts owed to you and minimize the risk of default;
- How to charge the right price for your goods and services;
- How to decide whether an investment will be a good use of your company's money or not;
- How to work out when, during each month, you 'hit the front' and start being profitable;
- How to set powerful and meaningful targets that will focus the attention of both yourself and your staff on making good decisions and taking positive actions ALL the time;
- A way to measure and track your financial success in a simple and meaningful way; and

- How to eliminate the unproductive habits that have been holding you back.

You will learn all this through the stories of my clients. Powerful stories about real business owners, just like you, with common financial problems. I'll show you how these business owners found themselves in trouble, how they worked out what was wrong (with a little help from the financial numbers) and how they took action to turn things around.

This book is not another one of those 'finance for non-finance' books full of indecipherable financial statements and scary calculations. In fact, this book contains less actual calculations than any other business finance book on the market.

I encourage you to read the stories, learn the lessons ... and have a bit of fun discovering how *Financial Foreplay®* can get your business to show you more love!

CHAPTER 1

The Secret to Never-ending Satisfaction

Finding the sweet spot in your business...

In This Chapter

"A visionary company doesn't simply balance between idealism and profitability: it seeks to be highly idealistic and highly profitable. A visionary company doesn't simply balance between preserving a tightly held core ideology and stimulating vigorous change and movement; it does both to an extreme."

Jim Collins

Serge was very proud of his café. I could see why when he showed me around in the week before it opened. Serge had a strong belief that for a café to succeed quickly, it needed to look 'serious' right from the start. He had invested heavily to achieve this. The tables and chairs were in place, the drinks fridges were already well-stocked, the kitchen was ready to roll with both equipment and non-perishable supplies. Serge had hired three staff members and spent a week training them to ensure a smooth opening. Any customer walking in the following Monday lunchtime would be forgiven for thinking this café had been running for a year rather than a few hours.

Getting to this point hadn't been easy. Serge had drawn down on his mortgage and used his considerable persuasive skills to convince his bank that an overdraft was necessary. Between these two actions he had generated enough cash to pay for his initial rental period, the fit-out of the restaurant and staff wages for the first fortnight. He'd talked his way into a 30-day account with the drink and snack distributor which had allowed him to stock the shelves. He'd also done a deal with a coffee company to supply him with a free espresso machine and a first batch of coffee that didn't need to be paid for two weeks. He had deliberately avoided using his credit card because he knew he would still need to buy a supply of fresh food just before opening.

But although things were tight, Serge wasn't particularly worried. He had a big business background – he'd worked in sales for the past decade

– and he understood the importance of Profit Margin. He had carefully calculated the prices on his menu to make sure they would be profitable. His well-practiced spreadsheeting skills had been tapped to ensure all his costs – including wages and rent – were included in the prices of his products. Finally, he had used his knowledge of marketing to build a real sense of anticipation about his café in the local community. Serge was confident that, from day one, he would be running profitably.

The next week, as he had expected, the opening was a success. He and his staff found themselves working hard within just a few hours. Serge was thankful that he had stocked up so well and trained his staff before the big day. By the end of that first day, he was already on the phone to all his suppliers ordering new stock; he was pleased to be able to pay them directly from a bank account freshly topped-up with the day's takings.

While business continued strongly, cracks were starting to show when I called to see Serge at the end of his first month. I found him sitting in his office, papers spread all around him and his costing spreadsheet open on the computer in front of him. He looked up with a frown.

"I can't work it out," he said. "I know that we're running profitably. I've been over my calculations a few times and I can see that for every meal we sell, we take in more money than we spent on putting it together. But I still have all these bills in front of me. I have to pay the staff again. I have to pay the coffee account. I have to pay the rent. And even though I've included all these things in my profit calculation, I'm still bumping up against my overdraft limit and struggling to find the money to make all these payments."

He looked back at his spreadsheets with a confused look on his face. "How can I be profitable and still have trouble paying my bills?" he said, partly to the computer and partly to me.

"It's actually quite simple," I replied, drawing a look of doubt from Serge. "You've fallen for the same trick that many small businesses fall for, especially early on. You've confused Profit with Cash Flow."

Serge looked confused. "There's a difference?" he asked.

Getting to First Base: Profit is Pointless... Cash Flow is King

Understanding the importance of Cash Flow, as opposed to Profit, is absolutely critical to running a successful business, yet it is often overlooked. In fact, more businesses go bankrupt due to a lack of Cash Flow than for any other reason. If you can grasp the difference between Profit and Cash Flow and become a master at finding and keeping cash in your business, success will be inevitable.

The common assumption is that if, like Serge, you are running a business in which the price you charge for your products is greater than what they cost you, everything will be okay: you will be profitable and successful. Profit is good – don't get me wrong – but it is not enough on its own. To be sustainable, your business must also have a healthy *Cash Flow*. Let me explain.

Every business has two young 'employees' whom you never see, but who are as important as any others. The first is an 18-year-old woman – we'll call her Penny – and she gets her energy from *spending*. (That shouldn't be too hard to imagine.) The second is a 19-year-old man – we'll call him Ernest – and he gets his energy from *earning*. As the business's cash registers and bank accounts swell, Ernest's stamina increases. Penny and Ernest are good reliable employees – you can be sure they will be with you for the life of your business, and, being imaginary, you don't have to pay them. The main problem with the pair is that they are constantly courting each other: they love playing that cat-and-mouse 'come and get me' type of chasing game.

Before a business opens, Penny, powered by all those start-up expenses, runs off. The more money spent, the further she runs. Penny beckons playfully back to Ernest, urging him to chase. He wants to run and play, of course, but he can't – not until the business starts bringing in some money. Only after the lights have been turned on, the coffee machine fired up and the first customer has paid her bill can Ernest take off in pursuit of his girl. His aim is simple: to catch Penny and, with plenty of silly laughter between them, to do, well, whatever it is that young men and women do when they are in love and chasing each other. It's all good, clean fun – but the business owner does need to keep these games under control lest they get out of hand.

Now an important thing to realize about Penny and Ernest is that their respective energy boosts – from spending and earning – only come from money *physically* leaving or coming into the business. This might be in the form of cash, bank transfers, incentives or rebates. Penny and Ernest do *not* get any energy from credit-related transactions until those transactions are settled. So Penny doesn't get an energy boost when Serge buys his coffee on a 14-day account; the spending boost comes when he pays the coffee account. Similarly, Ernest wouldn't get any extra momentum if Serge gave a customer a week's credit; his power would come when the customer settled up.

In other words, Penny and Ernest are only affected by what accountants call 'cash'.

Let's revisit Serge's situation. Recall all the money he had to spend before he started. Fitting out the café, paying rent in advance and paying wages to his staff while they trained. By drawing down on his savings and overdraft, Serge paid for these in cash. As a result, Penny was able to run a long way before opening day, giving her a good head-start on Ernest.

Things started to change immediately after Serge served his first customers. We know that the nature of a café is that most of its revenue is received as cash over the counter, so Ernest was able to start chasing Penny straight away. We also know that Serge had done his calculations and that his prices were high enough to cover his costs: he was earning at a higher rate than he was spending. So Ernest not only started chasing Penny, but he had more energy than her and started making up ground from the beginning.

However – and this is the bit Serge didn't see coming – combined with a good head-start from all that early spending, Penny had some additional sources of energy up her sleeve. Just as her stamina started to flag – as spending started to slow a little – Serge ran up against his first round of bills. After two weeks, his first coffee account was due and another round of wages had to be paid. More spending, and Penny was off running again. Shortly afterwards, the initial account of his drink and snack distributor was also due, as was another rental payment. More push for Penny. By the end of the first month it was clear that, while 'spending Penny' slowed down from time to time, she wasn't going to stop running.

It was a positive that Ernest kept on running also, as customers continued to come through Serge's door. His café quickly built a solid word-of-mouth reputation. But this wasn't proving enough to prevent much head scratching in Serge's office.

Serge's problem was that although Ernest was, on average, catching up to Penny, he wasn't doing so quickly enough. And in the meantime, Serge had to keep spending. Supplies had to be replenished quickly and constantly. No sooner was one bill paid than another – often bigger – took its place. The only way that Serge could spend what he needed to was to operate close to the limit of his overdraft, with his credit card as backup. And both these lines of credit had their own costs, in the form of interest, which Serge had not factored into his costing calculations.

Serge was becoming as confused and frustrated as Ernest would have been, had he been a real life boy chasing a real life girl for all this time.

KEY POINT

Regardless of your Profit Margin, cash coming in must exceed the cash going out at any point in time.

When Serge showed me his accounts, he was able to demonstrate that, on average, Ernest was catching up to Penny slowly: his overall 'cash in' exceeded his overall 'cash out' by about 10% per month. His business was operating 'profitably' in this sense. But I had to point out to him that no matter how profitable his day-to-day operation, he would not be making a real profit until Ernest caught up, and in fact overtook, Penny. At that point, his start-up expenses would have been paid off and sales income would exceed expenditures (including covering all his upfront bills). In the meantime, he needed to be able to keep spending on stock, rent and wages etc – to keep feeding Penny – or the whole game would come to a very abrupt halt.

KEY POINT
You cannot take profit to the bank and save or spend it. Profit is meaningless unless it is accompanied by underlying positive Cash Flow.

It took some time for all this to sink in for Serge. In his former, large corporate life, things had seemed more simple – from his point of view at least. His job had been to sell products for an amount larger than their 'standard cost' – the bigger the Profit Margin the better. What he hadn't properly realized was that behind the scenes in this large company was a finance department which had responsibility for managing Cash Flow. He hadn't needed to concern himself with it. Now, as a small business owner, he was his own finance department – both Cash Flow *and* Profit Margin were his responsibility.

At this point Serge and I wrapped up our first conversation about Cash Flow. I asked Serge to give some thought to how he might improve his situation. On returning the next day, his answers proved to me that he had understood some, but not all, of the concept.

Don't Come on Too Strong

Instead of invoices, Serge's desk was covered in newspapers. He was on the phone when I arrived, clearly talking advertising rates and negotiating in his highly enthusiastic way. By the look of the notes in front of him, Serge had already called a number of papers and, no doubt, struck attractive deals with each. As I waited, I noticed a sandwich board leaning against the office wall, ready to be placed out the front of the café. Chalked on to the board, in large letters, was: "COFFEE AND CAKE ONLY $5".

Oh dear, I thought.

Serge got off the phone looking pleased with himself. He always seemed in his element when driving hard bargains.

"I've thought about what we discussed," he said, "and as far as I can see there is only one solution. Even though we got off to a strong start, we have to increase sales even further. I know that my margins are profitable, even if we aren't making a 'real' profit yet. So it's simple: I need to sell more. The more I sell, the quicker your friend Ernest will run, and the sooner he'll catch up to Penny."

Well, I thought, at least he took the Ernest/Penny analogy to heart.

Serge went on quickly: "I've been in touch with all the local papers and organized some great advertising. We'll have half-page ads in all the main ones for the next month. Most of them will also do a 'review' – which I get to write! – because I'm going to spend so much with them. And did you see the sandwich board? I was just about to take that outside. Lots of other cafés around here offer these sorts of coffee and cake combinations at a discount, so why let them take my potential customers? I reckon we'll see an increase in Ernest's speed as early as today."

"Serge," I said quietly. "Do you think we could grab one of your corner tables and have a coffee?" My low-key response had the desired effect: Serge's enthusiasm immediately started to ebb away.

"I can see you've given some good thought to getting Ernest running faster by bringing in more customers," I said once we were sitting together. "But it probably won't work out just as you've planned."

I went on to explain that there were two major flaws in Serge's plans. Both were errors that I have seen made many times.

Serge's first problem related to his idea that simply increasing sales, by increased patronage, would speed up 'earning Ernest' sufficiently to catch his girl. The issue was that he had forgotten to consider the impact on 'spending Penny' of the changes he proposed.

First, Serge had committed to spending a substantial amount of money on advertising in order to increase the number of customers. This was money he was not already spending elsewhere, that is, it was new spending. Sure, he could probably buy the advertising on account, but that was irrelevant. Whether immediately or in a few weeks, this extra cash would need to be found, helping Penny run faster. (For the moment I spared Serge the discussion about the fickle nature of advertising and its lack of guaranteed success.)

Second, but on a similar note, an increase in Serge's turnover (assuming no other changes) would increase the amount of stock he would need to buy and, probably, the number of staff he would need to hire. Again, there would be an increased need to spend, helping Penny to run faster.

In short, Serge's plan to increase sales revenue (helping Ernest to run faster) would see Penny running faster too. What's more, the new spending on advertising would reduce his Profit Margin, making the task of catching up even harder for Ernest.

Serge's face dropped as the implications of what I was telling him started to sink in. It dropped further still when I pointed out that, quite possibly, carrying out his plan might see him run out of cash – and therefore go out of business – more quickly than if he did nothing.

KEY POINT

Increasing sales will not improve a Cash Flow shortage if the increase in revenue is cancelled out by greater spending to achieve the increase in sales.

"Okay," Serge said gingerly, after a few minutes. "What about the coffee and cake combination. Surely that's a simple enough plan to work?"

"I'm afraid not, Serge," I replied, "and you should be able to see the problem with this one yourself, given your understanding of the importance of Profit Margin. How much do you normally charge for coffee and cake, without the discount?"

"$7: three for the coffee, four for the cake," he said. "But not a lot of people buy both. So I figure if we can get an extra two bucks out of a few people, we'll come out ahead. The cake only costs me $2 a slice, so at worst we get extra cash in for no extra cash out, and some of the customers will no doubt buy some other things as well, boosting sales further. I know this won't get Ernest running much faster, but it shouldn't make Penny any faster either, should it?"

I had to acknowledge that on the basis of margin alone, Serge's thinking had some merit. I have had many other clients who give discounts which result in actually making a loss on some of their products. But I had to point out that Serge was still misunderstanding his central problem: a lack of Cash Flow.

"Do you see that by effectively giving away the cake for what you paid for it, each boost in Ernest's speed will be matched by an identical increase in Penny's. The end result will be no net change, assuming you do not have to hire extra team members to serve up the additional coffee and cake. And if the combination leads to better sales of other products, you're back to the same problem we have just been discussing: sales which you don't have the cash to support."

KEY POINT

Discounting is bad for your Cash Flow – it rarely has the desired effect.

(If you would like to see some numerical examples of how discounting prices affects your bottom line, refer to the Businest® website. In some cases, just a simple discount of 10% can result in you having to double or triple your sales in order to come out further ahead.)

"So what should I do," asked Serge with exasperation, "apart from cancel all that advertising I just booked?"

"What you need to do," I explained, "is increase your focus on Cash Flow, while maintaining your profitability. You need to give Ernest a chance to catch up to Penny – not by speeding Ernest up, but by slowing Penny down. Even if that means slowing Ernest down a little bit."

"You're saying I might need to reduce my sales rather than increase them? That, I have to say, is a bit hard for an old sales rep to swallow!" said Serge.

I understood Serge's difficulty with this, but it was important for him to get the point. Sometimes being successful in business means being counter-intuitive.

We knew that Serge had a positive Net Profit Margin so that, given time, his revenue – his Ernest – would eventually catch up to his spending – his Penny – and all would be well with the world. But because of the head-start that Penny had been given, and because he had left himself little room to expand his debt in the short term, it had to be accepted that Ernest's chase was going to take some time.

Possible actions Serge could take included:

- Making sure there was no unnecessary spending in the short term
- Subtle price increases in selected areas which would have little or no impact on sales (speeding up revenue – Ernest – without increasing spending – Penny)
- Negotiating extended payment terms with suppliers (This only delays the boost to Penny's energy, but it is a viable approach in Serge's case, where Net Profit Margin is positive.)

When is it PC to Talk about P&C?

What's the difference between 'Profit' and 'Cash Flow'? Remember that the money movements represented by Ernest and Penny are *cash* movements: *real* money moving in and out of a bank account and/or cash register. That's a good thing, because it means that when a business's earnings, represented by Ernest, finally catch up to and pass the business's spending, represented by Penny, then the resultant cash surplus is a *real* profit – one you can see reflected in your bank account.

In most businesses the accounts show things a little differently. Most businesses use what's called 'accrual' accounting (or what some jokingly refer to as 'cruel' accounting). Rather than record spending as 'money spent', they record spending as 'money spent *plus* money committed to be spent'. So if, for example, some stock has been purchased on account, accrual accounting includes the value of that purchase from the point it is made – not from the point when the account is paid. To use the Penny analogy, accrual accounting looks at how far Penny has run so far, then adds the distance she will run on energy she has already taken on board but not yet used. The same thing happens in reverse with earnings. Accrual accounting records earnings as 'money received *plus* money owed (expected to be received)'. When a sale is invoiced with 30 days to pay, the value of that invoice is included in accrual earnings even though the money won't be received for another 30 days (at least). In this case, Ernest is attributed all the distance he has already run, plus the distance he is expected to run using these 'outstanding' earnings.

When most accountants talk of 'profit', then, they are usually talking of '*accrued* profit' as opposed to what we called '*real* profit' above. Accrued profit is the expected real profit after 'spending already committed to', and 'earnings expected to be received', are taken into account along with real (cash) spending and real (cash) earnings. Rather than the difference between Ernest and Penny now, '*accrued* profit' is the expected difference between Ernest and Penny at some time in the future, when all outstanding debts and credits have been settled. You will see that a profit showing on your Income (or Profit and Loss) statement, in this sense, is a much more complicated – and arguably less 'real' – representation of the current financial situation of a business.

In practice, it is usually wise to have an eye on both your real profit (also known as your 'cash balance') as well as your accrued profit. It is a common error to focus on accrued profit only – an error which has the potential to send a business to the wall prematurely – and well before anyone expected.

Serge's café business was simpler than many in that its revenue was predominantly cash over the counter. The majority of businesses make their sales on invoice, for future payment, which adds a layer of complexity. (We're going to discuss this further in Chapter 3 when we discuss 'Receivables'.) But the basic rules of Cash Flow remain, and the basic game of 'earning Ernest chasing spending Penny' still needs to be managed.

If You Want a Date, You Have to Ask
(aka Remember to Invoice)

When I first met Jason he was excited, to say the least. His start-up business was going great guns and, apart from a few minor issues he wanted to talk to me about, the future was looking as bright as his eyes.

Jason had started his domestic electrical business as both an escape from the constraints of working for someone else, and as a way of giving him and his wife, Amy, the flexibility to support managing a family. For five years Jason had been a maintenance electrician at a large food factory. There was no problem with the work, but the rotating shifts – day shift one week, afternoon the next and then a week of nights – were really getting to him. Not to mention the constant rounds of job cuts and never knowing whether it would be his turn next. Amy had a secure job as an office manager with a construction company so the couple was comfortable that they could ride out any temporary dip in their income.

Getting set up had been straightforward. Jason and Amy had solid savings behind them and with the various equipment Jason had collected over the years – including his van – he didn't need to invest a lot at the outset. A bit of sign-writing and a few ads in the local paper and he was away. Amy was able to tap into her established networks for a few clients to get Jason going, and with that start he went from strength to strength. Jason immediately enjoyed the variety of running his own business, and they both appreciated his ability to work something close to 'normal' hours.

As Jason's business grew he wondered why he hadn't made the change years before. His only concern was that, despite his success, the credit card was running at its limit and it was getting harder to pay the bills. He couldn't understand why this was happening, which eventually prompted him to look for some outside help.

As it turned out, it was lucky he did. If he hadn't, he would have been out of business, or refinancing his home mortgage, within a few months.

ꕥ

On the surface, Jason's business was simpler than Serge's. His original start-up costs were low, so his 'spending Penny' should not have been able to get much of a head-start to his 'earning Ernest'. Provided he was charging his customers the full value of any hardware he bought, plus a fair rate for his time, he should have found his Ernest catching up to his Penny quite quickly. But this wasn't happening. Much as had happened to Serge,

Jason was clearly having problems with his Penny (spending) getting too far ahead of his Ernest (earning), leaving the latter tired and frustrated.

The day I met Jason I joined him in his van as he went about his work. Our first call was to his local wholesaler from which he needed to pick up some parts for the day's jobs. It was fairly routine stuff – even I knew what most of the products were: various power-points and other wall outlets, a few light fittings and the like. I had noticed that there didn't seem to be a lot of stock in the back of the van, and Jason explained that he preferred to buy most of his supplies as he needed them. (A big tick right there, I thought to myself.) And besides, he went on to explain, he didn't have much spare cash to stock up anyway.

Jason had an account with the wholesaler which had to be squared up monthly. This had worked well early on, but now in his third month he admitted he was concerned about making the next payment. Something wasn't adding up, but for the moment I let that comment go.

We pulled up to the first job – a simple installation of a replacement fan in the customer's main bathroom. With the owner's permission I went in as well, though I did feel a bit awkward – I was hardly dressed as a tradesperson. The job was done quickly and I trailed Jason back to his van. He opened the center console of the van and pulled out an invoice pad. I noticed that the pad – a simple hand-filled duplicate pad – was quite thick though nearly used up. On the first blank form, Jason scribbled out a description of what he had done, along with his customer's details. He tore off the original and returned to the house to leave it with his customer.

In the few moments that he was gone, I flicked through the duplicates in the pad ... and saw immediately where Jason's problem lay.

"Jason," I said as he got back into the van. "I notice there are no prices written on these invoices. How do people know how much to pay you?"

He laughed. "Yeah, well, I haven't been doing this long enough to know all the prices off the top of my head. So I just write out what I've done, then take the book back to the office where Amy helps me match up these duplicates with the receipts from the wholesaler. We then use that information to produce proper invoices on the computer which we post out to our customers."

I asked the next question tentatively, even though I had a good idea what the answer would be. "How often do you do that – the reconciliation and the invoicing?"

"We try to do it at least weekly," he replied, "though I must admit we've got a bit behind. The matching-up takes ages, and we're still learning how to use the bookkeeping software so invoicing has got beyond us too."

I flicked through the book again. "So would you be two, maybe three weeks behind with your invoicing?"

"Yeah, at least that," he said. Then, after a few moments: "Probably a month, come to think of it. We've been pretty busy. Did I tell you Amy is pregnant?"

He hadn't, so I passed on my congratulations. Then I launched into my Penny and Ernest story. It turned out that Jason's situation was quite simple after all, but it had become more complicated because, to use our analogy, he had taken his eye off Penny and Ernest and forgot to focus on his Cash Flow.

As I mentioned before, Penny had not got much of a head-start in Jason's case as setting up his business did not require a lot of funds. His situation was helped even further by his main supplier – the wholesaler – being willing to extend credit to him right from the start. In effect, Penny had hardly run any distance at all in the first month of Jason's operation. Penny's first real push-along didn't come until the end of that first month, when his first wholesaler account became due. At that point Jason's spending became a bit more serious.

Meanwhile, Jason's 'earning Ernest' could have been well underway in his chase after Penny from very early on. Within a few weeks, Penny and Ernest could have been cuddling up to each other and working together on a profitable enterprise. But they weren't, for one simple reason: Jason hadn't been invoicing his work. Effectively, he had done nearly all his work for free, with a promise to invoice, but then left the invoicing for weeks. His customers were 'lucky' if they saw an invoice within a month of having had work done. With the usual delay between invoice and payment, Jason wasn't actually being paid for his work until around two months after the job. Rather than closing the gap (catching up with 'spending Penny'), 'earning Ernest' had hardly left the starting line.

KEY POINT
No one pays without an invoice, and until you get paid, you are out of pocket for the invoice amount, your time and the cost of the materials. Forgetting to invoice is a little bit like wanting to go out on a date but never bothering to ask.

Thankfully Jason didn't take long to understand what I was telling him. His problem wasn't that he was stupid – he just didn't understand the priorities. Coming from his background – a big factory where getting paid just wasn't a concern of the maintenance guys – the 'Penny and Ernest' game wasn't something he was familiar with.

And we had caught the problem in time. We agreed that Amy would take on the role of invoicing outstanding work and following up previous invoices that had not yet been paid. Together, Jason and I created a simple table which helped him convert time spent on a job into billable dollars. He then used this table, along with his wholesaler invoices, to hand-write invoices – including dollar amounts – at the time he did the jobs. With new clients, he asked for payment on the spot, by cash or check. With existing clients, he continued to offer credit, but offered a 5% discount for immediate payment.

Before long, all Jason's clients were paying him immediately on completion of work. Amy took on the task of banking checks daily. Within a month or so, his Ernest was running as fast as ever. Better still, because he was being paid for the hardware he used before he had to pay for it himself (by paying his account in 30 days), his earning Ernest was running *ahead* of his spending Penny. Jason found himself in the ideal business situation of having money come in before its related expenses go out.

Your Bookkeeper Is From Mars and Your Accountant is From Uranus

We will come back to concepts of spending and earning, profit and cash – and Ernest and Penny – many times during the rest of this book. But before we move on, let's have a very quick overview of where we're going.

After Jason and I had talked invoicing – following my discovery of his invoice book in the van – Jason quizzed me about the idea of Cash Flow. He was a keen learner. He now understood, courtesy of his harsh lesson, that 'doing profitable work' was a very different thing from maintaining a workable Cash Flow. He also understood his limitations as a small business operator who, like so many others, had started his business without any real training. And he wanted to avoid, if he could, making more 'classic' mistakes in the future.

I explained to Jason that even though his bookkeeper or accountant never discussed these important issues with him whey they reviewed his financial statements, there are four broad areas that could have an effect on his future Cash Flow:

- The first is **Inventory**. *Increasing Inventory reduces Cash Flow.* "Imagine," I explained, "that instead of buying your supplies as you need them, you stocked up your van with 'some of everything' so that you only had to go the wholesaler once in a while. Do you see that doing that would mean spending a lot of money?" Jason nodded and I went on: "Increasing Inventory is like giving energy bars to Penny while weighing Ernest down with a heavy pack. Penny would race ahead (energized by the money spent on the new Inventory) while Ernest, for reasons I'll explain later, would quite likely slow down eventually." We will discuss the effect of Inventory on Cash Flow in more detail in Chapter 2.
- Next is **Receivables.** *Increasing Receivables – the amount of money owed to a business – also reduces Cash Flow.* This was effectively Jason's problem because he wasn't getting his invoices out; the more common situation, I explained, is where invoices have been sent but aren't being paid on time. "In either case, Ernest

is held back – not by losses but by a failure to turn work done into cash. Remember that Ernest can't move until the cash comes in. Meanwhile Penny continues to race ahead as money is spent on fresh supplies so that new work can continue." We'll look at Receivables and their impact in Chapter 3.

- Third are **Payables** (and GST payments). *Increasing Payables – the amount you owe others – by holding back payment increases Cash Flow.* I told Jason about Serge and why I had encouraged him to negotiate longer payment terms with his suppliers. "When payment is delayed, the effect is to slow down 'spending Penny'. It doesn't remove her energy for good, but it does delay her ability to use it. Meanwhile, Ernest powers ahead (hopefully) on the revenue earned from sales, closing the gap between him and his girl." The smaller the gap, the greater the Cash Flow. Jason eventually learnt this once he had his invoicing in order. With his payable terms on his wholesaler account at 30 days, and his receivable terms as cash-on-delivery, his cash revenue quickly outstripped his cash spending. We'll investigate Payables in Chapter 3 also.
- Finally, there is **spending on Assets** (which accountants call 'Fixed Assets'). *Spending money on Fixed Assets decreases Cash Flow,* at least in the short term. Assets are listed by accountants separately from Inventory because they are 'permanent' as opposed to the transient nature of stock. The effect on Cash Flow of buying an Asset is similar to the effect of buying Inventory but more detrimental. Spending on a major Asset is much like starting up another business. The challenge is similar to what was faced by Serge: how to deal with a large up-front expense which turns into a big head-start for 'spending Penny'. I asked Jason to think about what would happen if he were to buy or lease a new van. He would need to make sure that the extra spending wouldn't harm his healthy cash situation by draining cash from his business. This is a more complicated topic which we'll return to in Chapter 5.

Elsewhere in this book, we'll look the other important areas you need to manage in order to run a sustainable and profitable business. These include **Pricing** (Chapter 4), managing **Costs** (Chapter 6), achieving your **Break-**

even (Chapter 7) and managing **Debt and Equity** (Chapter 8). We'll finish off by looking at the ways you can use **Measurement** to help you manage all these things (Chapter 9), and ways to get the best out of yourself (Chapter 10).

But to reiterate the main point I've been trying to make in this chapter. The distinction between Profit and Cash Flow is absolutely critical. **Failure to understand the difference, and failure to detect and fix negative Cash Flow issues, are the main reasons why most small businesses fail.** Nothing could be more deserving of your time and attention. The payoff is HUGE. Finding hidden cash in your business and putting it to work today will enable you to succeed in any economic environment and reward yourself with a much deserved pay increase.

Whip Your Business Into Shape NOW!

The Secret to Never Ending Satisfaction – Give Your Bank Balance a Dose Of Viagra!

- It is important to look at your financial statements each month. As a minimum, you need to view your Income Statement (or Profit and Loss), Balance Sheet, Aged Receivables and Aged Payables reports
- Cash Flow is easy to calculate:

  PROFIT +/- Inventory changes +/- Receivables changes +/- Payables (& GST changes) +/- Fixed asset changes = **CASH FLOW**

- Check your bank account. If you don't have any money in it and are constantly relying on credit, this is a good sign you have a Cash Flow problem that must be addressed quickly
- Tips to increase earning and make Ernest run faster:
  - ✧ Brainstorm ways to increase sales without discounting or incurring costs (e.g., advertising) to do so
  - ✧ Stop discounting
  - ✧ Calculate how much Profit Margin you are making on everything you sell – more on this in Chapter 4
  - ✧ Work out where you can increase prices without having a negative impact on sales
  - ✧ Collect all money owed to you – more about this in Chapter 3
  - ✧ Investigate ways to get paid immediately (COD terms)
- Tips to slow 'spending Penny' down:
  - ✧ Re-negotiate better supplier terms
  - ✧ Minimize unnecessary spending on Fixed Assets. Before you invest in plant and equipment, determine how much sales will have to increase before you pay off the item. More about this in Chapter 5
  - ✧ Order only as much inventory as you absolutely need. If you can get new shipments of stock in 3-5 days, there is no need to have 3 months worth of sales sitting on your shelves – more about this in Chapter 2
  - ✧ Cut unnecessary expenses

CHAPTER 2

The Big Release!

The #1 pent up frustration in your business

In This Chapter

WARNING: Inventory May Be Killing Your Business

Why STD's Are Bad for Business

Unlock the Big 'O' and Maximize Satisfaction!

Why Shrinkage is Just as Much a Problem for You as it was for *Seinfeld's* George Castanza

Chapter 2 - The Big Release!

"It is vain to do with more what can be done with less."

William of Occam

Charlie loves his hobbies. He loves meticulously building scale model cars, running toy trains to tight timetables and bringing radio-controlled airplanes in with perfect landings. He especially loves finding something rare, like that Airfix Handley bi-plane he stumbled across recently, over 50 years old and still sealed inside the factory's bag! That discovery really made his day.

It will come as no surprise that when Charlie got the chance to buy his own hobby shop, he jumped at it. He poured his love of hobbies into the store. He chatted intently with his customers, giving them as much dedicated, old-fashioned service as they could bear. He prided himself on his ability to track down the most obscure model or part, no matter how old. He prided himself even more on stocking an enormous range: it was rare that a customer would come in and not be able to find what they wanted. On the rare times that Charlie took some time off, his 'holidays' would be spent scouring toy shops and op shops, always on the lookout for a particularly fine die-cast tractor or slot car that he didn't already stock. When he found something, he would buy it and display it proudly in his shop ... until the next holiday. Then a new stock of rarities would arrive and anything left over from the past year was put away, well, wherever he could find a space.

When I first visited Charlie's store, I wondered if I was too late. Perhaps his business had gone under before I'd had the chance to help? There were so many boxes stacked up in the shop that I thought he was packing up to move out. But I was wrong. Charlie's shop was literally packed to the rafters with product.

Charlie himself was serving a customer when I arrived so I had a look around. From floor to ceiling, every shelf was neatly but tightly stacked with models, kits and games. Between the shelves, down the middle of the aisles, were more boxes. These were mostly shipper boxes which were not yet unpacked. They were piled so high that I had the feeling I was exploring a maze. The further back in the shop that I went, the darker and dustier it got as the box 'skyscrapers' got taller and taller.

When I sat down with Charlie a few minutes later, I asked him one of the first questions I ask all my clients: "How much stock to you have?" Unsurprisingly – I've seen this many times before – Charlie looked around slowly as if noticing the piles of stock for the first time.

"I have no idea," he said. "Why, does it matter?"

"Because if you had less stock," I said, "you probably wouldn't need to be talking to me about how to keep your business from going bust."

WARNING: Inventory May Be Killing Your Business

Inventory is one of the great hidden costs of business. Very few business owners understand its importance or, more to the point, the importance of keeping it under control. Inventory increases spending (speeding up your 'spending Penny') and ties up your cash while providing little or no benefit to revenue. In fact excessive Inventory can weigh a business down – imagine Ernest becoming more and more overweight – and ultimately lead to revenue losses.

Excess Inventory is so often the cause of business Cash Flow problems that it is often the first thing I look at after I enter a business as a consultant. And it's why you should have a clear understanding of how much Inventory you have, what it's worth, and how old it is.

I opened this chapter with the story of Charlie's hobby shop because it is a prime example of Inventory gone wrong. His business exemplified the three main areas in which Inventory can cause problems:

First, Charlie had no discipline for controlling how much stock he bought, and he almost always decided his purchasing volumes based on quantity discounts. As a result, Charlie's store was packed with multiples of identical items, many of which he might sell, if he was lucky, one each year. The rest were left to gather dust while increasing his overdraft. In a minute we'll meet another of my clients, Carol, who was also affected by the drive to take advantage of discounts.

Second, Charlie's store was so crowded, and his wallet so empty, that he was no longer able to buy more stock. While he could offer a customer any of the scale model planes released five years ago, he didn't have stock of the newest, just released models. He simply couldn't afford to buy them, and had nowhere to put them. After a time, customers grew to understand that if they wanted the latest (which was most of them), they needed to go somewhere else. As a result, Charlie was losing customers and sales.

Finally, Charlie's store was so dark and crowded with dusty boxes that, most of the time, he had no idea whether anyone was in the store. He suspected – in fact he knew – that some of his smaller items would disappear into a pocket from time to time but he could never catch anyone. A greater source of shrinkage than theft was breakages. Because his boxes were packed in so tightly, the older ones on the bottom would eventually give way. When this happened, numbers of cartons would crash to the floor leading to inevitable damage. Such stock just had to be thrown away. While he knew there was theft and breakage-related shrinkage, Charlie had no chance of knowing how big the problem was. His stock was so extensive that he had no hope of counting it regularly. At the end of this chapter I'll tell you about Pamela, another client who was affected by shrinkage.

Why STD's Are Bad for Business
(aka Why You Want To Avoid the Bulk-Buy or Supplier Trade Discount)

A few years ago I had a client, Carol, who ran a beauty salon. Carol had built a busy business, with a solid base of customers who returned at regular intervals. But she had a costly habit.

One day I arrived to find Carol counting the stock on her shelves before placing her next order. I told her I was impressed to see that she had a bit of a system to this – that she wasn't just ordering off the top of her head. She went to stop, so we could talk, but I encouraged her to keep going. I wanted to see what happened next.

After Carol had finished her stock count, we went back into her office. Strewn around the desk were a number of flyers advertising monthly specials from her suppliers. This will be interesting, I thought to myself. Carol moved methodically down the list she had just made. For each product, she hunted around on the desk until she found the corresponding supplier's brochure, then she used that brochure to work out how many of that product to order. Every time, her decision was guided by what discounts were available – not by how many of the item she already had. So for one particular type of shampoo, for instance, Carol's list said she had five in stock. The flyer for that shampoo offered a 10% discount for orders of 30 bottles or more, so she ordered 30.

"How many bottles of that shampoo would you sell each month?" I asked.

"Oh, five or six," she replied.

"So, the 30 bottles you are about to buy, plus the bottles you already have, will cover you for about six months?"

"Yes," she agreed, "but if I don't order them now, I won't get the discount."

It was time for a heart-to-heart. I explained to Carol that buying bulk goods because they are on special is one of the worst financial crimes that one can commit in their own business. Taking out my notepad, I listed the problems she was creating for herself one by one.

First, I pointed out, Carol was spending money a long time before she would earn anything from it. This would suck cash out of her business, and could well find her taking out a loan or drawing down on an overdraft to keep things moving along. This point was reiterated for me when we were interrupted by one of Carol's staff members looking for some hand-cleansing lotion: there was none left. Carol told her assistant she would deal with it and asked if I would walk with her down to the supermarket a few doors down. On leaving the supermarket, I asked Carol why she had pulled out a credit card to pay the cashier. Her answer was that she didn't have the cash at the moment – that she needed what was in the till to pay the staff.

"How will you pay for the stock you are ordering now, including those discounted shampoos?" I asked.

"I'll probably have to use the card for those too," she replied with a sheepish grin. "I've had to do a bit of that since I stocked up on new hair colors a few months ago."

"And what interest rate are you paying on your credit card?"

"I think it is 20% at the moment," said Carol.

The math was conveniently easy. I explained to Carol that the 10% saving she was making on her shampoo by buying a six-month supply was directly offset by the 10% interest (ie, half of 20% per annum) she would pay on her credit card over the same period.

"So ... ," Carol responded, half to herself, "with the 5% discount I received on the hair colors – which will also last me six months – it will cost me more to borrow the money needed to pay for the stuff than I saved with the discount."

"You got it!" I exclaimed.

KEY POINT

Avoid the seduction of cheap supplier temptations – borrowing money to access a bulk discount will cause you to wake up in the middle of the night for all the wrong reasons.

But Carol's Inventory problems didn't stop with the cost of borrowing money. I asked her to think about the product she was intending to buy in bulk. Did it have a use-by date? She explained that it didn't really go 'off', but that the product, being aimed at the fashion market, often changed its packaging. In fact, she realized as she spoke, there was a good chance that the reason the discount was being offered was because they intended changing the packaging quite soon.

"So if they change the packaging before you sell all of this stock, you'll be stuck with old product. What normally happens," I asked, "when you get stuck with old product?"

"I end up either giving it away or selling it at a discount," she said. "I guess I would quickly lose the benefit of having bought it cheaply if I had to do that, wouldn't I?"

KEY POINT

Every bulk order introduces the risk of product going past its best-before date or otherwise being superseded before you get the chance to sell it. When this happens, it nearly always offsets any benefit gained from buying in bulk in the first place.

I liked working with Carol. She was quick to understand lessons like this, and she was always willing to learn from her mistakes.

Before we moved on, I asked her add up the cost of the bulk stock she intended to order. The total amount equated to about two weeks' turnover. After she verified that all the products she kept on hand could be re-supplied within a week if necessary, I asked her to calculate the cost of a smaller order – this time for only what she really needed over the next couple of weeks. This time the cost of the order came to one-tenth of the first order – about one day's takings.

Spending some time on her books over the next couple of hours, I was able to demonstrate to Carol that taking the 'small order' approach – and thereby spending money more slowly – would quickly allow her to pay off her credit card and get back into the 'black'. That's the magic of keeping Inventory levels low.

Every time you buy stock for your business – raw materials or saleable product – you should see the purchase as an investment. Like any other investment, you should expect it to provide you with a financial return in a short time. So Carol buys shampoo from her wholesaler because she expects to sell it to her customers at a price greater than she paid for it, and thereby make a respectable profit on the transaction. Simple? Yes. But it gets more complicated if there is any significant gap in time between when you buy the goods and when you turn them into cash by selling them and collecting payment. These buying/selling gaps are widest when you buy products in bulk because it will necessarily take you longer to on-sell the goods you've bought. And the longer you keep them, the greater the risk that you won't be able to sell them at all, or at least without heavy discounting.

When you spend before you earn you are effectively taking out a loan for the intervening period. Very often this will require a 'real' loan from some sort of finance company (in the form of, say, an overdraft, or a credit card debt as in Carol's case), a delay in paying suppliers or, perhaps more seriously, a delay in paying yourself. This is similar to buying bulk groceries for home using a credit card in the hope that you'll get your next pay before the credit card payment is due, only to find that some perishables go off before you've actually paid for them.

If you are lucky enough to have cash to make a bulk inventory purchase, you obviously won't need a bank loan but you will be, effectively, taking a loan *from yourself.* In the next case study I will explain what I mean by this.

Unlock the Big 'O' and Maximize Satisfaction!
(aka Avoid Missing Opportunities Because You Don't Have the Cash to Invest.)

Byron is one of my more interesting clients. He is in the business of collectables. His store is a sort of antique shop but rather than selling furniture he sells 'things'. His shop is packed with wonderful old items: everything from classic painted biscuit tins to old petrol station signs to 100-year-old woodworking tools to, perhaps most interesting of all, old guns. In many ways Byron is similar to Charlie, the hobby shop owner we met earlier. He lives for his business because it gives him the chance to make a living out of doing what he enjoys most: collecting.

When it comes to running his business, Byron is a bit of a traditionalist. He keeps a fairly tight rein on his finances and rarely, if ever, borrows money. I don't think he even owns a credit card. Financial conservatism doesn't vaccinate a business against potential financial problems though, as Byron found out just before he called me. He was struggling, he explained on the phone, because he was running out of cash and was unable to buy new stock. This was a real problem because the strength of his business lay in constantly having new items to show off. New stock encouraged his customers to come back often; no new stock meant they would tend to check out his competitors first.

The challenge for a collector like Byron is that he likes to, well, collect. And what he collects is often governed more by emotion than it is by assessing an item's value as an investment. Byron isn't silly. He won't buy items for his store that he doesn't think someone will like, and buy, at some stage. It's just that he doesn't always consider how far into the future 'some stage' might be.

When I first walked into Byron's shop, one of the most obvious items was a beautiful old gun, proudly (and securely) displayed in a glass cabinet. I couldn't help but ask how much it was worth. Clearly proud of his fine exhibit, he explained that he had bought it for $5,000 dollars, but was looking to sell it for $7,000. Following a hunch that I had hit on his problem straight away, I asked Byron when he had bought the gun. He didn't remember exactly, he said, but thought it was about five years ago.

I asked Byron how many other, similarly high value items he had in his store. We went for a walk and in the course of showing me around, he pointed out at least a dozen items which he had bought for over $5,000 over the last few years. In each case, he was quick to tell me how much he was intending to sell the item for, and the margin was always 30 to 40%. But the fact was – and I didn't point this out to him just yet – he hadn't sold these items, so at the moment they were costing him money and, most importantly for Byron, causing him to miss the opportunity of buying new stock.

It was time to get to work. I sat Byron down in his office and explained to him a few facts of financial life.

The main thing Byron needed to understand was that *all* Inventory has a cost. If you don't borrow money to buy it (as Carol was doing in her salon), then the cost is what is usually called an 'Opportunity Cost'. It is a cost of lost opportunity. Byron had spent nearly $100,000 on expensive items a few years ago. The items were attractive and valuable, but they weren't particularly rare, so they weren't appreciating in value significantly. In effect, then, Byron had put $100,000 on the shelf of his office and left it there for all that time. In other words, while he wasn't borrowing money from the bank, in effect he was borrowing it from himself. He had missed the opportunity of investing that money somewhere where it would give him a solid return, such as in a term deposit or in blue-chip shares. And now he was missing the opportunity of using that money to buy smaller, less expensive items that he knew would sell quickly.

KEY POINT

If your Inventory is not turning over regularly, it is a liability not an Asset. Money spent buying Inventory – even if it isn't borrowed money – has a cost. That cost is an *Opportunity Cost:* the cost of not being able to use that money more productively and profitably.

After working with Byron for a while, he eventually understood the concept of Opportunity Cost and we worked together on finding ways to improve Byron's situation.

The first thing he did was to free up some cash by actively selling some of his more expensive items. He used online auction sites and his own 'collectors' network to find buyers. In some cases he had to sell the items for a little less than he had intended, but the benefit was cash in his pocket. In every case Byron found doing this difficult – some of these items had been with him for so long that he saw them as family! – but he was now starting to understand the difference between being a collector and running a collectables business.

The next thing Byron needed to do was set up some systems to keep better track of what stock he was holding. He started with a major stocktake, recording everything in the store. At the same time, he started recording the *age* of all the items in the store – not the product's age itself but the length of time he had held it in stock. We agreed that in future, any item that had not sold after one year would be reviewed. Byron would investigate the item's market value and decide whether or not it was increasing in value sufficiently to be worth keeping. If not, he would act to move the item on.

After a few months, Byron was making much smarter purchasing decisions. He was still enjoying 'collecting' for his store, but his focus was different. His focus was less on attractive, expensive but not-so-rare items, and more on smaller items he knew he could sell quite quickly. To his pleasant surprise, he found that using this strategy, he was able to do more shopping rather than less, because he had more cash available to spend. And he was able to do all this without having to get himself a credit card!

☙

Even the best run businesses are prone to losing out to Opportunity Cost. If you don't have a clear idea of how much Inventory you have, and how quickly it is turning over, this could be you. Yet keeping track of your Inventory situation is easy to do. Later we will look at how you can do this, but for the moment, the important thing to do is to understand that all Inventory costs you money, whether you buy it on credit or pay for it in cash.

Why Shrinkage is Just as Much a Problem for You as it was for *Seinfeld's* George Castanza

I was a little surprised that mobile food vans could be so lucrative. I'd had a call from Pamela, who owned *Pam's Pantry*, and the initial turnover numbers she shared with me were higher than I expected. Nevertheless,

Pamela's business had started to struggle and she couldn't work out why. Turnover remained high, but her profit seemed to be falling back, and she had noticed a lower than normal cash balance at the end of a few successive weeks.

After spending a day with Pamela out on the road, it was easier to see where the money was coming from. New factories and small businesses had sprouted all over the suburbs in which she worked. The growth had been so rapid that essential services like food stores had simply failed to keep up. With many businesses a good car ride from their nearest take away shop, they relied on food and drinks coming to them. Pamela was only too happy to oblige.

Pam's Pantry had started with one van, driven by Pamela herself, but quickly developed. She now had six vans operating across a large part of the city. She had decided, for the time being, not to go down the franchise route. Rather, she leased the vans herself and employed staff to operate them. As the business had grown, Pamela's initial approach of picking up supplies directly from her suppliers quickly became inefficient. Instead, she found a small warehouse which included a coolroom and had suppliers deliver their goods to her.

My initial thoughts on visiting Pamela were that the warehouse might be where her problem lay. Very often, businesses operate like family homes: the more space you have, the more space you use. So I imagined that leasing herself a place to store Inventory would have led to Pamela buying up plenty of stock. Like Carol in her beauty salon, Pamela would have been tempted regularly by bulk-buy offers – not for the fresh food she sold, but for things like chocolate bars, chips and soft drinks.

It quickly became clear, however, that excessive buying was not Pamela's problem. From previous experiences working in a large distribution company, she understood the principles of inventory control and keeping her stocks to a minimum. Nearly all the stock her business owned was kept 'active' in the sense that it lived on the trucks. She kept four or five days of non-perishable supplies in the warehouse; she saw this as helping with efficiency because her drivers could load up these products each evening before going home, pack fresh food first thing in the morning then get out on the road. Pamela monitored fresh food quantities closely and ordered according to proven sales patterns. By the end of each day, there was very little fresh food left on any of the vans.

Pamela kept a fairly close eye on her cash situation too. Hers was a cash business: there were no accounts and the only method of payment was in notes and coins. Each vehicle was provided with a float in the morning, all sales were recorded and the tills were reconciled at the end of each day. The vehicles themselves were leased on competitive terms so they did not tie up excessive financial resources either – Pamela had done everything she could to avoid the sorts of Opportunity Costs I found with Byron.

In short, this seemed to be a business under control.

But, as she'd told me on the phone, Pamela's profit was falling away and she couldn't work out why. And nor could I, for a little while, until I started helping Pamela do some sums on her purchasing figures.

After looking at the value of goods bought every week, over a two-month period, and comparing that number against sales for the same period, it was quickly obvious that while sales stayed roughly the same, Pamela was spending more and more money on supplies – particularly the non-perishable supplies. The amounts weren't huge, but they were increasing consistently, to the point where expenditure had crept up about 5% over the past six weeks.

We checked her invoices to see if the wholesale prices Pamela was paying had changed over the period in question, but they hadn't. In fact Pamela was a canny operator and had convinced her major suppliers to keep most prices frozen for three months at a time. So 'price creep' was not the problem.

This left only one likely culprit, but before telling Pamela what I thought it was, I needed a couple of questions answered.

"What system," I asked, "is in place to keep track of stock levels in the warehouse, in each of the vans and between the two?"

"I have to admit that there is no real system," she replied. She understood the need to keep track of stock, but this was one area where she had not yet had time to do anything. And anyway, she figured, the business was pretty simple. The only way stock could go missing was if it was being stolen. This was unlikely. The vans weren't like convenience stores where customers could easily pocket a chocolate bar without anyone noticing. They had small service counters which were supervised by her drivers at all times. What's more, because her customers were all gainfully employed, they wouldn't be interested in pinching stock anyway. "I guess I have faith in the basic honesty of people and haven't felt the need to tighten up in this area yet."

"How long have your drivers been working with you?" I asked.

Pamela was quite relaxed on this question. "I use an agency and they assure me that they do thorough reference checks. So far I've been pretty lucky. Five of the staff have been with me for nearly a year. The last joined three months ago."

While Pamela didn't think stock loss – otherwise known as 'shrinkage' – was likely to be a problem, I felt it was the only area left that we hadn't looked at in detail. It seemed to me that shrinkage was the primary area not under control. And by this point, unfortunately, I had a fair idea where the problem was likely to be.

Giving away as little as I could, I suggested to Pamela that she count the warehouse stock each day for the next week, and that she also count the stock on one of the vans as a starting point. I suggested that she do this on her own and reconcile her findings against the sales records for the sample van. A quick look over the vans suggested that the newest driver was the least organized so I thought her van would be the best place to start.

To cut a long story short, Pamela was *un*pleasantly surprised by what she found – and my suspicions were proved correct. While the stock in the warehouse seemed to reconcile correctly, the sample van – that of the newest staff member – did not. Quite simply, more stock was leaving the van each day than was being sold, and the difference had to be going somewhere. After checking and then re-checking the numbers, Pamela had no choice but to confront her staff member who admitted to taking "a couple" of bars of chocolate and packets of chips home "from time to time". Because it wasn't being monitored, she had somehow got the impression that it hadn't mattered. As it turned out, this employee's minor thefts may not have been noticed except that the more she took, the more confident she got and the larger her thefts became.

In the end, the police became involved and Pamela learnt a valuable lesson about stock control.

KEY POINT
Stock shrinkage will, eventually, become a problem for your business if you don't have tight control over your Inventory.

No matter how honest you think your customers and staff are, shrinkage is a common problem. Failure to monitor stock movements carefully can send you out of business quicker than a knock at the bedroom door by one of your children can ruin an intimate moment. The less control you have over your stock, the higher the likelihood of shrinkage. Those who are inclined to 'take something home without asking' will normally start small, but their 'borrowings' will slowly increase to whatever they feel they can get away with.

The only way to find these problems early is to have good knowledge, at all times, of your Inventory situation. Regular stocktaking and reconciliation is essential, as is an appropriate level of security.

And before you say "but my staff are trustworthy", answer this question of *yourself*: have you ever, at any time in your life, taken home a pen, ruler or other piece of stationery ostensibly because you didn't think it mattered? If you have – and nearly everyone has – then you should see my point. Understand that a 'meaningless' pen for one person will be an 'inconsequential' weekly chocolate bar for another and an 'insignificant' carton of shampoo for someone else.

Inventory shrinkage is a widespread problem – perhaps as widespread as more prominent forms of late night shrinkage – and it deserves to be taken seriously.

Before we wrap up this chapter, let's quickly revisit Charlie in his hobby shop. Remember that Charlie had managed to be touched by all of these problems with excessive Inventory. He had bought quantity discounts and cluttered his shelves with multiple copies of models which only ever sold slowly. He was missing opportunities to buy new stock because of his cash shortage, and as a result was losing customers. And his shop was so messy and crowded that although he knew some of his stock was being stolen, he was powerless to do anything about it. Added to all these problems, Charlie had no real idea of what stock he did have so he had no way of telling whether these problems were getting worse or not.

I worked with Charlie for some time and helped him address each of these problems.

He started by having a large sale and by advertising some of his rarer products online. He discounted heavily for this sale, but we decided the discounts would be worthwhile in this instance to both clear the floor and the overdraft, and to free up cash. With the resulting cash, Charlie was able to refresh his catalogue with newer, more popular items. On the back of his strong reputation for service, it wasn't long before most of his old customers were coming back – often. And after the big sale and clean-out, the hobby shop was cleaner, lighter and more organized. From the counter Charlie could again see most of the store and discourage further theft. At the same time, breakages were all but eliminated, thus reducing another source of shrinkage as well. And, finally, we set Charlie up with a regular method for counting and monitoring his stock levels and age so that he could avoid getting into the same predicament again.

With the changes made, Charlie was able to free up cash, pay off his overdraft and help ensure that he was able to keep selling hobby supplies for many years to come.

When I last called Charlie, he was at a model train convention.

Whip Your Business Into Shape NOW!

The Big Release – How a Quick Reduction of Inventory can Release a lot of Pent-Up Tension and Frustration!

- Prepare a spreadsheet that lists all the stock items you sell, ranking them in order from what you sell the most of per month, to what you sell the least of
- Determine minimum stock levels on all items (use the amount you sell each fortnight or month as a guide)
- Take a good look at the items on the bottom 60% of your sales report – could you sell these off right now to generate some much needed cash?
- By and large, 80% of your sales will come from the top 20% of your items. Examine your list and ensure that you are carrying enough, but not too much, of these top-selling items
- Put a simple system in place to count your stock regularly and reconcile any differences that exist between what you have, and what you think you should have
- Put a simple system in place to ensure you (or your staff) are only ordering what is absolutely necessary
- If you do not have sufficient cash in your bank account to pay for stock, avoid buying in bulk to obtain a discount
- Set timeframes for selling stock that is of high value or has a use-by date. Record the age of stock and revisit the list regularly to ensure that stock gets sold before it becomes useless
- Monitor the cost of your Inventory each month. The easiest way to do this is to track the cost as a percentage of sales. If this percentage starts to increase, you will be able to see it immediately and take action to protect your profitability and Cash Flow. More about this in Chapter 4.

www.businest.com

CHAPTER 3

Building Commitment Without Being Taken for Granted

The hidden romance killer in your business

In This Chapter

Are Your Debtors Just Not That Into You?

Payment Speaks Louder Than Words

Pay Me Now Or Pay Me Later

How To Know When Your Customers are Leading You On...

"I can't give you a surefire formula for success, but I can give you a formula for failure: try to please everybody all of the time."

Herbert Bayard Swope

Turning a passion into a business is something many people dream of doing. Sam was one of the few who had managed to make this happen. Photography had initially been a hobby for fun but had graduated to serious hobby, then become a part-time 'job on the side' and finally become a full-time business. By the time I met her, Sam's business was in its third year.

Sam had just established a nice new studio inside a restored period house. As in most photography studios, very large, glossy examples of her work lined the walls. There were gorgeous portraits of mothers and babies, fashion shots with stunning models and, of course, a number of wedding photos. There were also examples of a recent foray into commercial food photography. There was clearly no shortage of talent here.

As we chatted it was clear that Sam's passion and enthusiasm was as strong as ever. She had big plans for her studio and big plans for the food side of things. There was a boom in the publication of cookbooks and she felt well placed to take advantage of it. As a food lover as well, it seemed a natural fit. And there was another advantage, Sam felt: the opportunity to deal with professional, corporate clients who knew what they wanted and were prepared to pay for it. This, unfortunately, was not the experience she often had when dealing with individuals – especially bridezillas on wedding shoots!

However, dealing with corporate clients had its own complexity. Where nearly all the personal work was paid for up-front (with clients paying for the shoot then paying for the pictures they wanted), corporates expected to be provided with invoices on 30 day, and sometimes 45 day terms. In other words, corporates wanted Sam to do the work and be paid for it later. Sam didn't have a problem with this generally – she knew it was standard business practice. The problem she did have, and the reason she'd asked me to see her, was that in reality it was taking her much longer – sometimes as much as four months – to get paid.

Until recently, Sam had seen this tardy payment of her invoices as an annoyance. There wasn't any significant impact on the operation of her business. As a service business, her clients were paying mostly for her talent; the cost of things like processing and printing were quite small compared to the fees she charged. She didn't have any trouble covering her rent or the lease payments on her equipment. But lately Sam was having trouble paying a salary to herself, and that was hurting.

Are Your Debtors Just Not That Into You?

Sam was not alone in needing to learn this basic yet important business lesson. It is quite common, in my experience, for owners of small but growing businesses to find themselves out of their depth as their relationships with their customers change from small and cash-oriented to larger and invoice-oriented.

I started by telling Sam about 'spending Penny' and 'earning Ernest', about the need for Ernest to keep up with Penny generally, and about the importance of Ernest catching up to and passing Penny over time. Sam found this analogy fairly easy to get her head around. I had to agree when she suggested that in a small service business like hers, with relatively low outgoings, a tight coupling of Penny and Ernest was less critical than it would be in larger businesses or businesses with higher levels of Inventory.

I went on: "Your relationship with Penny and Ernest does change, however, when you start providing your clients with credit. And that is exactly what you are doing when you move from taking all payment as cash, at the point of delivery, to invoicing and accepting payment at some specified time in the future.

"When you give credit, you are accepting a degree of risk and giving away control over your Cash Flow. It's as though you're starting to treat Ernest as a more trusted employee (he's the one authorizing the credit to various customers). You're more willing to let him go off on his own, and willing to accept the risk that something could go wrong. Your expectation is that this sort of delegation will make you and your business more flexible, attractive in the marketplace and productive overall. A similar thing happens in reverse when you start paying for goods or services on credit: you are giving spending Penny more leeway and accepting the risk that she could get ahead of herself. (See the section below on Payables – 'Payment Speaks Louder Than Words') Again, you do this in return for a payoff in terms of flexibility and productivity."

I explained to Sam that Ernest and Penny are like any 'real life' employees to whom you delegate more influence: that delegation needs to have boundaries, and those boundaries need to be managed. There need to be some checks and balances.

"Imagine that Ernest and Penny's relationship outside work has grown with your business," I said to Sam. "So at this stage, as your business is starting to mature and move into a new phase, so is their relationship. They're starting to go out on regular dates. Most of the time, Ernest, being an old-fashioned guy, commits to picking Penny up from her apartment. But before long there is a problem. Ernest keeps turning up at the agreed time, but he consistently finds that Penny isn't ready for him. Over time, he finds this more and more frustrating."

"Just like my customers!" Sam exclaimed. "I do the right thing and efficiently invoice them straight after the end of each job, but when it comes time to pay, they're not ready – they hold me up. It's very frustrating for me, too."

KEY POINT

When extending credit to customers, systems need to be put into place to make sure that credit is controlled and that invoices are paid in a reasonable time (or credit may be refused in the future).

Sam understood exactly the point I was trying to make. I asked her what she would suggest Ernest might do to improve his situation.

"I guess I'd suggest a few things. He might try calmly explaining his frustration to Penny – better communication can often remedy these sorts of problems. He might try calling ahead to warn Penny that he is on the way in the hope that she might get ready earlier. He might try some sort of incentive system: perhaps rewarding Penny with dinner at her very favorite restaurant if she could be ready three times in a row. Or, in a worst case scenario, he might simply lay down the law and tell Penny that if she can't be ready in a reasonable time, he'll stop picking her up at all."

These were good ideas, and very similar to the sorts of things Sam could try in her business to manage her 'Receivables' – or outstanding invoices. We talked about a few, all of which Sam put into place over the coming months.

The first thing Sam did was similar to the 'call ahead' strategy. She made a point of calling any client whose invoice hadn't been paid by the due date. She did this regularly and immediately: the call was made on the day immediately after the invoice was due. This tactic had an immediate effect with some clients, who either started paying on time without being asked, or at least made the payment (or a part payment) as soon as they received Sam's call.

Sam's second approach was the 'improved communication' strategy. With more troublesome clients – often some of her larger corporate clients – Sam spent some time on the phone tracking down the specific person who was responsible for initiating payment of her invoices. Having found that person, she made polite enquiries about the money she was owed. Over time, she found that by building some rapport with that person her payments started to be made more quickly. It was strange, she told me once, but it seemed that even 'faceless' large corporates had a tendency to pay the people they liked ahead of those they didn't.

There was a third strategy in Sam's kit which she saved for particularly troublesome clients. It was the equivalent of Ernest's 'I won't go out with you anymore' approach. With these clients, Sam instigated a 'stop credit' policy. While remaining polite, she simply explained to these clients that she could not do any more work with them until all their outstanding invoices had been paid. In one case she went further and stopped providing credit altogether – all future work was done on a cash-on-delivery basis only.

> **KEY POINT**
> **A combination of strategies may be needed to ensure invoices are paid on time. These can range from improved communication to stopping of credit. Different approaches can be chosen for different situations, but all should be applied consistently.**

In combination with her debt-chasing strategies, there were two other things that I recommended Sam put into place. These were not tactics for chasing debt, but rather for keeping it under control. Similar to Ernest (subtly) keeping tabs on Penny. They were:

- An upfront credit check on all new clients who requested credit. This can range from asking for trade references, with whom credit history and reliability can be checked, to a request to review the potential client's most recent financial statements.
- Development and regular tracking of internal measures (key performance indicators, or KPIs) showing how much money is currently owed in outstanding debts over 30, 60 and 90 days. The Businest® website has a number of simple and powerful tools for tracking your key numbers and for comparing them against previous periods and industry benchmarks. This proprietary online software will help you quantify the cost to your business of not collecting your debts more quickly.

> **KEY POINT**
> **In addition to effective chasing of unpaid invoices, upfront appraisal of new clients along with regular monitoring of key measures will improve your Receivables situation immediately, and increase your Cash Flow.**

Pay Me Now Or Pay Me Later

There is another credit management tactic which Sam hadn't used but could have considered: the 'incentive' strategy. This involves providing some sort of incentive for early payment of an invoice. Such an incentive is often made in the form of a discount. A 2%, or even 5% discount might be provided for upfront payment in full, or for payment on time. (Occasionally these incentives are 'offered' in reverse, by way of a late payment charge of, say, 5% of the invoice. In my experience, late fees can be difficult to extract from clients, and they certainly have a more negative connotation than early payment discounts.)

When considering a discount incentive, the cost of that incentive should be compared against the likely benefit. Benefits include:

- The value of having the money in your bank earlier. This is a positive version of the 'Opportunity Cost' we learnt about in Byron's story in the chapter on Inventory. A calculator on the Businest® website can help you quickly compare the opportunity benefit of early payment with the cost of the discount. You may want to consult this tool prior to offering a discount to select customers to ensure that it will be beneficial to your business.
- The value of not spending your time, or a staff member's time, chasing outstanding payments. In businesses like Sam's, chasing debts can be both time consuming and stressful. (If your business is large enough to employ an accountant or bookkeeper, ask them to record, for a period, how much time they spend chasing outstanding payments. This will give you some idea of the cost of all this effort.)
- Reduced risk of bad debts. Every business will run up against this eventually: the company that simply won't pay its debts or which goes out of business with debts outstanding. Of course debt collection and legal opportunities exist to chase such debts, but the cost of such actions will often outweigh any benefit. So if in doubt, encouraging payment before you start might be to your advantage: better to receive 90% than nothing!

One thing to think about when considering a discount incentive is this: you might choose to use it selectively. With reliable clients who always pay on time, there is little to be gained – and 2% or 5% to be lost – by offering a discount which you know they will take advantage of. You may want to offer the incentive only to your troublesome clients. Increasing their base fee by the discount amount is one way to do this fairly. I recommend referring to the early payment calculator on the Businest® website. It will help you to compare the proposed discount with the corresponding annualized interest rate. This will help you to assess whether it is beneficial or not for you to offer the proposed early payment incentive.

With some simple systems in place and a professional approach, it wasn't long before Sam's outstanding debt situation had markedly improved. She made the interesting observation to me that she felt she was treated better by her clients because they knew that they couldn't take her for granted. I pointed out that that sounded like the sort of respectful relationship that Ernest and Penny might have talked about over dinner one night!

Payment Speaks Louder Than Words
(aka Payables – an Often Neglected Source of Cash Flow)

There was another area that Sam was able to work on to improve her Cash Flow: her 'Payables'.

Payables are bills you have to pay at some point but haven't paid yet. Essentially, anything your business buys on account – either product or service – becomes a Payable at the time of the purchase. It's much the same as your power or telephone bill at home: the invoice comes with a due date some time in the future.

A Payable on your accounts is mirrored by a Receivable on the accounts of your supplier. Payables reflect Receivables in other ways, too. Just as reducing your Receivables Days (by getting outstanding invoices collected) increases Cash Flow, so does increasing your Payables Days. The longer you put off making a payment, the longer the related cash stays in your bank. Your Cash Flow goes up as a result.

As Sam became better at managing her Receivables, she also started to be more careful with her Payables. She had prided herself on paying bills as soon as she could. She felt this was 'nice', and she also liked keeping things tidy by not owing too much money at any one time.

At one point in our talk about Receivables I had to share an awful truth with Sam: that business is not about being 'nice' – it's about being business-like. "Your corporate customers aren't holding back on paying you because they want to be nasty. They are just being smart with their money by holding on to it for as long as they can. When they do this across the board, they end up with quite a large amount of cash sitting in their businesses which wouldn't be there otherwise. What you need to do is think like a big business: don't pay invoices until they fall due.

"I loaded it on Penny a bit in my earlier example," I went on, "but we could just as easily turn the tables and have Ernest as the 'problem child' in the relationship. How would Penny feel if Ernest consistently turned up late? Every relationship is a two-way street." Sam told me that from her own bitter experience she knew exactly how Penny would feel.

There are businesses which have a policy of not paying any invoice until they are hurried up by their supplier. As many companies, especially smaller ones, are not good at following up, this tactic can add a number of days to the average Payables Days. This is not an approach I would necessarily endorse. It can give you a bad reputation over time and reduce the scope for cooperative relationships. On the other hand, no one is going to reward you for paying your bills before the due date.

To improve her Payables management Sam did three things.

The first was to stop being 'nice'. She held back on her Payables until the due date, and within a few weeks she was already noticing the higher level of cash which was flowing through her business.

Her second step was to apply the same logic, but in reverse, to early-payment discounts on Payables as she had with Receivables (see box above). Before accepting a discount for early payment, she made a rough calculation of the value of holding on to the money for the full term allowed by the invoice, and then compared this value with the benefit of the discount. Often the discount was worth pursuing, but not always. It was worth the small effort to do the calculation.

Finally, when negotiating pricing arrangements with new suppliers, Sam started to incorporate payment terms into the discussion. Her strategy was to get the best price she could, then stretch things further with longer payment terms where she could. When she did this, I could see that she was really behaving like a business person now. It was good to see!.

Receivables tend to get most of the attention in discussions about Cash Flow, mainly because they need closer attention. It is hard to get Payables wrong – unless you overlook paying altogether. But there can be substantial Cash Flow benefits to be had by stretching out your Payables.

How To Know When Your Customers are Leading You On...

Any teacher will tell you that it is a wonderful privilege to watch someone grow from a tentative newbie to a confident contributor to the class. Business coaching is no different. While the coach, like the teacher, understands that their own role is only ever a small part in a student's success, there is, nonetheless, immense pride in seeing success blossom.

So it was with Craig and Mandy. The couple had started out much like the electrician Jason and his wife Amy, whom we met in Chapter One. After training as a plumber, Craig had worked for a time with a building firm before branching out on his own. Mandy took on the very-much-part-time job of doing the invoicing.

One Friday afternoon a couple of years later, Craig was chatting over beer with some mates. The talk was upbeat. One of the blokes worked for a developer which had just won approval for a large project: a 200 unit retirement village. As the talk went on it was suggested that Craig should bid for the plumbing work and, to cut a long story short, he did so ... successfully. Almost overnight, Craig went from being a one-man-band who used the occasional contractor to being the manager of a serious plumbing business. Soon after, Craig rented office space and Mandy joined the business full-time to oversee the administration side of things.

From there, it was onwards and upwards for Craig and Mandy. One contract led to another and before long they were managing three or four major jobs at a time, along with various smaller jobs given to them by their developer clients.

It was hard to reconcile the pair as the same naïve, inexperienced young couple who had sat in on one of my business coaching workshops only a few years before. All the signs were that their business was successful, and it was – but for one thing. Mandy was concerned that despite their accounts showing significant profit, she was starting to have trouble paying the bills. It was another case of strangled Cash Flow.

Very often when I visit a client for the first time in a while, I feel like one of those forensic experts on CSI or one of those other television shows focusing on the solving of obscure crimes. Thankfully – for me and also for you, as a business owner – finding tell-tale wounds in a business is usually simpler, and considerably less messy, than doing an autopsy on a corpse. And my patients tend to still be alive, even if somewhat bruised and battered, when I get to them.

Being a larger business, Craig and Mandy's case was more complicated than Sam's. My first hope was that, as former 'students' of mine, they hadn't got themselves into trouble with something as basic as a failure to invoice. That lesson – which Jason learnt in the earlier chapter – had been drilled into this pair a long time ago. And, sure enough, when Mandy and I sat down she was able to assure me that her invoicing was up-to-date. She spent a lot of time on the back of Craig's band of trades people and none of them dared go home without leaving completed job sheets, detailing work to be invoiced, in the in-tray.

The next symptom of strangled Cash Flow which needed to be ruled out was excessive Inventory. Again, Craig and Mandy had been well trained to avoid this. Supplies were generally bought as required and almost everything that went into a van was destined for a particular job. Mandy had developed a simple but effective labeling system so that any stray stock could easily be identified, and she watched this closely.

So now we had to explore a bit deeper, and that meant delving further into the financial numbers of the business. We took a scalpel to the business's 'Receivables' and on opening them up the source of Craig and Mandy's problem quickly became clear.

I asked Mandy if she remembered 'earning Ernest' and 'spending Penny' from the work she'd done with me previously.

"Aren't they those invisible employees who are always playing games chasing each other?" she replied. "When Ernest catches up to Penny, our business is in the black."

"That's right. You can put it another way, though. A shortage of cash means that, somehow, Penny has managed to run ahead of Ernest. You need to close that gap – the gap between bringing money in and spending it."

"But I thought Ernest ran faster the more we 'fed' him. So the more I invoice, the faster he should run. And I've been doing plenty of invoicing." Mandy looked confused.

At this point it was clear that Mandy had forgotten a critical point about Ernest: that his energy doesn't come from accrued revenue but from real revenue, that is, cold, hard CASH. I set about explaining the difference to Mandy.

When you raise a typical invoice, you are asking for payment at some time in the future. It might be 30 days hence, 60 days, 90 days or something else. Your accountant will call that amount a 'receivable': a debt owed to you by customers where payment is to be received down the track. Your accountant will also, probably, mark the amount of that invoice down as revenue because it is pretty much guaranteed that it will come to you eventually. But, importantly, none of this makes Ernest run faster: he doesn't do that until the money owed to you has been received into your hot little hands (or at least into your hot little bank account).

The same thing happens with Penny. In Mandy's case, she had a 30-day account with their major plumbing supplier. Stock bought for a job didn't have to be paid for until 30 days after it was supplied. So, again, on the day that Craig and his staff bought supplies, their purchases didn't make Penny run any faster. Rather, Penny stored the ability to run faster – she accrued the 'payable' amount – for 30 days.

Imagine for a moment that Ernest and Penny now begin to carry small backpacks. When an invoice is raised for future payment, Ernest stores the appropriate amount of energy in his backpack; he uses that energy when the bill is finally paid. When stock is purchased on account, Penny stores energy in her backpack which she uses when the account is eventually settled.

"What we have here," I explained to Mandy, "is a case of Ernest taking advantage. He's not taking advantage of Penny though ... he's taking advantage of *you*."

In Mandy's case, her invoices were issued on 30-day terms: she expected they would be paid 30 days later. This matched nicely with the 30-day terms she was being given by their supplier. All being well, Craig and Mandy's business would pay for the supplies used on a job at the about the same time they received payment for that job. Imagine Ernest and Penny skipping along together, side-by-side and hand-in-hand. But this isn't what was actually happening.

Looking at Mandy's accounts in detail, her 'Receivables' were sitting at 80 days. In other words all her requests for payment in 30 days weren't actually being paid, on average, until after 80 days. Quite a large number of invoices – worth nearly $500,000 in total – still hadn't been paid after 90 days. In addition to not having any money in the bank account, the business was incurring interest carrying charges of almost $1000 per month because they had to use their line of credit and credit cards to pay their wages and bills.

"Ernest has stored a large amount of energy in this backpack, but he's just not using it. He's hoarding, and he's slowing down from the weight as a result," I said. "In the meantime, Penny just keeps running. She *is* consuming all the energy you give her, because you're paying your bills on time. It is this difference in their speeds which is opening up that gap I mentioned before: the 'Cash Gap' between bringing the money in and spending it. As a result, it's getting harder and harder to pay the bills."

KEY POINT

Cash outlays must ideally be offset by cash receipts at the same time or earlier. When spending consistently occurs before earning, a Cash Gap opens up and, sooner or later, you run short of cash.

I could see that Mandy was starting to understand what I meant, but she was confused and a bit hurt. She prided herself on keeping on top of this sort of thing. "So how did I get into this situation?" she asked. She then proceeded to answer her own question. "It's not as though I don't spend time chasing up payment. We regularly follow up outstanding invoices. But now that we are dealing with large clients – all these large developers – they just have so many reasons for *not* paying. Some of them are just so pedantic about paperwork!"

I asked Mandy what she meant by this and she pulled copies of a number of outstanding invoices from a large folder. As we went through them, there seemed to be three main reasons for delays in payment.

First, there were invoices which didn't include a client purchase order number. Some of Craig and Mandy's clients required that a purchase order be signed off by their head office, authorizing the work, before any work commenced. In most cases this was fine, but occasionally one of the plumbers was asked to do a small extra job while they were on site: installation of a dishwasher, or an external tap, or even just a change of washers. The plumbers, having been well drilled by Mandy, always wrote out a job sheet for these tasks, and they always had that sheet signed off by the supervisor on site. But, unfortunately, the developer's main office didn't regard Mandy's job sheets as purchase orders. Mandy's assistant spent a lot of time to-ing and fro-ing to have purchase orders raised retrospectively for this work. In the meantime, entire invoices – for both the 'unauthorized' work and the other 'authorized' work done at the same time – sat unpaid. (For a comprehensive checklist of the information that your invoices should contain - at a minimum - in order to maximize your chances of getting paid on time, refer to the Businest® website.)

A second, though related, source of payment hold-ups was disputes about whether or not work had been done. Most of the time this was, again, a paperwork issue. Larger clients required that all invoices be accompanied by matching job sheets for all work, signed by both the tradesperson and the onsite supervisor. In general this worked well, but, as supervisors usually worked on more than one job at a time, they were not always around when the job sheet needed signing. Mandy would often take a call from a frustrated plumber who was due at another site but had just spent half-an-hour trying to track down a supervisor for his autograph. Sometimes she had to let the plumber bring the form back unsigned, even though she knew that from the point of view of the developer head office, this would count as 'work not yet done'. Once again, entire invoices would be held up while the paperwork caught up with what had happened in the real world.

Finally there were disputes over quality. Though often minor, Craig would have to personally visit any site where the client was dissatisfied with work done. A tap slightly off-centre, a scratch on a toilet seat, a loose piece of roofing iron. Once a remedy had been agreed and actioned, there would be more paperwork before payment could be made. Once again, a large invoice, covering multiple pieces of work, could be held up by a dispute relating to just one task.

All these situations combined across a significant number of invoices and quite a few clients to create Mandy's Receivables back-log. It was like old tuna sandwiches were piling up at the bottom of Ernest's backpack, for weeks and even months on end.

☙

As I suspected, Craig and Mandy's situation was more complicated than Sam's. Mandy had exhausted most of the strategies used by Sam: rigorous follow-up, better communication and being the 'bad guy'. But her problem was different: her outstanding invoices were held up by bureaucracy rather than simple resistance to making payment. So a different approach was needed.

Mandy's answer was to separately manage the things she had control over and those she didn't have control over. Her most successful tactic was to break large invoices down into smaller ones, in particular invoicing separately any task for which she did not have complete paperwork. So an 'extra' job, missing a purchase order, would be invoiced separately from other work in the same location. Similarly, tasks with job sheets unsigned by the client were invoiced separately. This allowed the majority of invoices to pass smoothly through her clients' systems, while 'troublesome' invoices could be managed separately.

Jobs over which there was a quality dispute were more tricky because the problem usually didn't arise until after invoicing. For these, Mandy – who now had a bit more time up her sleeve – created a system of daily review which helped Craig to inspect and fix the issues more quickly and get the invoices moving again.

KEY POINT

Receivables management sometimes requires lateral thinking. Separating that over which you have control, from that which you don't, can be helpful to speed things along.

Not long after putting these ideas into practice, Mandy and I looked at her Receivables figures again and found she had made significant progress. In particular, her Receivables were now sitting at 40 days where they had previously been 80. Ernest was now able to use his 'stored' energy quickly and had closed the gap between him and Penny.

The final thing I needed to do with Mandy this time around was help her set up a better system for reviewing the state of her Receivables. It was because she wasn't tracking this that things had managed to get out of control in the first place. With new measures set up which Mandy could monitor every week, she was much better placed to retain control in future.

Whip Your Business Into Shape NOW!

Playing The Field – Expand Your Options to Maximize Your Pay Off

- Put a system in place to call and email debtors as soon as their invoices become past-due – and follow the system you have put in place
- Make available many possible payment types to make it easier for customers to pay – credit card, debit card, electronic funds transfer, check, cash, Paypal etc
- Get a commitment from debtors on the phone to have payment in full (or a part payment) by a specified date
- Build rapport with the individuals responsible for paying your invoices. Take a genuine interest in them and thank them for keeping your accounts up-to-date
- Institute a stop-credit policy for repeat offenders
- Do not be afraid to send debts to a collection agent or lawyer – it is better to get some of the money than nothing at all
- Put together a comprehensive checklist of information that you need to get from all potential customers BEFORE you make the decision to give them credit terms
- Develop standards and measures for what you will tolerate in terms of debts outstanding 30, 60 and 90 days – investigate what is standard in your industry
- Once standards are set, performance manage whomever is responsible for collecting debts in your company – this is one of the most important jobs in your business
- Consider offering an early payment incentive to customers who are chronically late but not delinquent
- Ensure your invoices contain ALL of the information required for you to get paid on time
- Follow up any discrepancies or disputes immediately
- Whenever possible take notes or get correspondence and promises from debtors in writing
- Set aside a specific block of time each week to review and follow up on outstanding debts
- Wherever you can, ask for payment upfront or on a COD basis
- Where jobs spread out over several months, ask for part payment each month to keep the Cash flowing in

www.businest.com

CHAPTER 4

Scoring Every Time

Finding the big payoff... guaranteed!

In This Chapter

Are You Chasing Customers Instead of Profitable Sales?

Keeping It Nice When Things Get Complicated

"The reasonable man adapts himself to the world; the unreasonable one persists in trying to adapt the world to himself. Therefore all progress depends on the unreasonable man."

George Bernard Shaw

Carlos and Frank were destined to work together from the time they started their apprenticeships. Theirs was one of those friendships that never needed to be talked about or actively nurtured – it was just there, as solid as if it were a third person. Their joint passions were for furniture building and fishing. After they finished their training they immediately paired up to establish a business, *Big Catch* Furniture, producing custom-made tables, bookcases, entertainment units and the like.

After 20 years the two business partners had built a solid reputation for themselves, while not setting the furniture world on fire (so to speak). They didn't try to win awards for design or test the boundaries of the trade. They had simply stuck to their goal of accessibility: they sold affordable products which were of good, solid quality but not top-of-the-range.

My impression on my first visit to Carlos and Frank's factory was that it was a model of efficiency. It was their third plant – they had outgrown the previous ones – and while there was obviously a bit of dust around, and the characteristic smell of cut timber filled the air, the place looked far more organized than similar factories I have seen.

It was Frank who showed me around. He was the talkative one, and these days essentially ran the front of the business: sales and administration. A couple of assistants helped him out with purchasing, invoicing and so on, and he used a part-time bookkeeper to keep the numbers in order. Carlos, preferring the company of his carpentry kin, ran the manufacturing side of things with half a dozen full time staff.

Carlos and Frank ran a fairly simple business. On the Inventory side, most of their furniture was made-to-order so they didn't seem to be at risk of holding too much finished stock nor work-in-progress. They kept some raw materials in the form of timber, but most of what they bought was fairly generic and readily available so they didn't need to keep much on hand. They bought their supplies on a 30-day account and, because most of their customers were individuals, their sales were generally Cash-on-Delivery – Receivables were not a constraint. Initially it was hard to see where they could be going wrong and why they would need the help of someone like me – though I knew from many past experiences not to take first impressions at face value.

After my guided tour of the factory, Frank took me into the showroom where we could sit and have a talk at one of the *Big Catch* dining tables. Like all the best businesses, the product seemed to exemplify the Carlos and Frank's values: simple and sturdy, but classically stylish at the same time.

Frank gave me the background to their decision to ask me to come and see them. "Carlos is a genius in the factory. He is constantly looking at ways to work more efficiently. He changes layouts to move related machines closer together and rearranges the way particular jobs are built. And he makes sure all his staff are trained to do everything, giving him maximum flexibility. He also measures nearly everything: he was able to tell me the other day that the factory's average productivity has improved by 10% in the past twelve months."

This, Frank went on to admit, was at odds with the way he tended to operate himself. Since he'd moved into more of a sales role, and away from Carlos's constant influence, he'd reverted to a more laissez-faire style of operating. He liked chatting to new customers and doing deals. He kept an eye, he claimed, on the 'big picture' of the financial numbers but preferred to leave the detail up to his staff.

"It was Carlos who had pointed out our problem – I may not have recognized it otherwise," said Frank. "He showed me that our Profit Margin in the last year was slightly lower than it had been the year before. But it should have been higher, given Carlos's improvements in the factory. He has decreased the average amount of labor going into each piece of furniture while our prices have stayed the same. That should be coming out the other side as extra Profit Margin, but it's not. The opposite is happening. And I don't know where to start to work out why."

"We'll probably be able to find out what's going on," I told Frank with a smile, "but I'm afraid it will require diving into the detail. We'll need to look at your GP, your COGS and some ABC analysis of your sales."

Frank rolled his eyes. "I don't think I'm going to enjoy this," he said, and then added, with a pleading look, "I'm just a simple furniture maker". I assured him that what we were going to look at was not nearly as complicated as it sounded.

Are You Chasing Customers Instead of Profitable Sales?

At their most basic, the concepts of COGS and Gross Profit should be fairly easy to understand for most business owners. When I translated the jargon I had just thrown at Frank, he agreed that it wasn't as scary as it sounded.

'COGS', I explained, stands for 'Cost of Goods Sold'. For a given product, it is the total cost of all the direct 'inputs' into that product. At *Big Catch*, these were essentially the materials (mostly timber) and the labor. A simple product like one of *Big Catch's* 'Everyday' coffee tables would have a low COGS because it didn't require a lot of timber, nor a lot of time to put together. Conversely, a more complex product, like one of their 'Blackwood' range glass-doored, hardwood wall cabinets with six drawers, would have a significantly higher COGS. There was more timber, of a better quality, in this product, and it took a lot longer to build.

"And we reflect that higher COGS in a higher price," said Frank a tad shortly, as if I was just stating the obvious.

"That's right," I replied, "but that's where the next key performance indicator (KPI), or important measure, 'GP', comes in."

'Gross Profit' (GP) is the difference between the sale price of a product and its COGS. Gross Profit is often expressed as a percentage – the 'Gross Profit Margin' (GPM) – to make comparisons between operating periods (ie, months or years) more clear. So a product which sells for $200 and has a COGS of $100 has a 50% GPM, whereas a product which sells for $120 with a COGS of $100 has a 16.7% GPM.

> **KEY POINT**
> **'Gross Profit' (GP) is the difference between the price a product is sold for and the direct costs associated with buying and/or making that product. The direct costs are known as the Cost of Goods Sold (or COGS).**

(Note that when we discuss Gross Profit and Cost of Goods Sold, we are ignoring, for the time being, all the 'behind the scenes' costs of things like rental, management and administrative wages, marketing expenses and so on. We'll come back to these Fixed Costs in Chapter 6. For now we are concerned only with the costs and revenue directly associated with producing products (i.e., Variable Costs).)

"Clearly," I went on, "a higher GP is better. And – at the risk of stating the obvious again – there are two ways to improve the Gross Profit of a product. You can increase the price while keeping the COGS the same, or you can keep the price the same and reduce the COGS."

"Which is where we should be seeing Carlos's efforts in the factory. He has reduced the labor input on average, so most products should have a lower COGS. Our prices haven't changed, so our overall Gross Profit should be higher, shouldn't it?" Frank was starting to get the idea. "So why is it lower?"

"Let's have a look at some of those numbers," I said. "Perhaps I could spend some time with your bookkeeper."

☙

Over a number of meetings, Frank's bookkeeper and I delved deep into the sales and financial numbers of *Big Catch* Furniture. It took a bit of time, mainly because we were starting from scratch.

Comparisons are critical. Every business is different, so while it is possible to use benchmark figures of things like Gross Profit Margin as KPIs, it is equally important to look at the change over time of Gross Profit and COGS, along with other factors like the mixture of products sold (percentage of high-end versus low-end Gross Margin products or services, for instance). Knowing and tracking your GP margin each month is very important. It can alert you to changes in your COGS so that you can make adjustments and corrections to your profitability. (The Businest® software will track these changes for you and provide you with easy to read reports and a clear summary of your most critical numbers.) Knowing these KPIs can allow you to make better decisions and focus your time and resources on work that will produce real results.

☙

When Frank and I sat down at the showroom table again some time later, I asked that Carlos join us so that both partners would get the full picture.

"Two things have happened here and, combined, they have had the effect of more than offsetting the gains Carlos has made in the factory.

"On one hand, the cost of most of your timber has gone up. The cost hike was greatest in the higher quality hardwood you use in your new 'Blackwood' range. The increase hasn't been huge – about 7% – and it has been gradual, which is why it may not have been noticed. But that increase has driven your COGS up while your production efficiencies were trying to drive them down."

I went on to explain that the other change was in the mixture of products sold – in particular the introduction of that new range.

"This new 'Blackwood' range has been quite successful, it seems?" I asked Frank. He agreed. Despite being their most expensive range, sales had been steadily growing since its introduction a little under a year ago.

"When you brought it in, how did you come up with prices for each of the products?"

Frank pulled out a price list. He showed me how the prices of the new range were about 10% higher than their previous 'premium' range. When pressed, however, he had to admit that no science had gone into setting these new prices. He had known the cost of the timber for this range was higher than their previous hardwood, but he wasn't sure how much higher. And he hadn't checked with Carlos that the labor input would be the same.

I looked at Carlos, who looked at his friend with a good-natured sigh. "Frank doesn't spend enough time with wood anymore. Every carpenter knows that blackwood is more time consuming to work with. Add the higher timber cost on top of that ..."

KEY POINT

Properly calculating the Cost of Goods Sold can be difficult and time-consuming. But to avoid doing so means you are flying blind and your prices are essentially guesses. This can be expensive and fatal to your business.

I didn't really need to say much more. Both Frank and Carlos clearly understood where the issue lay. The new range had a higher Cost of Goods Sold at the outset due to higher labor costs, but this had initially been disguised somewhat by Carlos's efforts to improve efficiencies. As the new range caught on and sales increased, overall COGS within the business had also increased. The higher price of the new range was initially sufficient to cover the COGS but eventually the rising timber price pushed COGS further up again. This increase in COGS, combined with the change in the mix of products sold (i.e., the percentage of high versus lower Gross Margin), pulled the Gross Profit Margin down.

Let's put this in the context of our faithful assistants 'earning Ernest' and 'spending Penny'. *Big Catch* Furniture was profitable: their Ernest and Penny were getting along famously. Carlos's improvements had reduced spending, slowing Penny down. But the increased cost of the new products *increased* spending: initially by a small amount but later by more as timber prices rose and sales of top end hardwood products increased. Overall, Penny was now running faster. And while the higher prices of the new range were pushing Ernest along too, his gain in speed was less than Penny's: Ernest started to have trouble keeping up.

Frank's next question was the obvious one: what could they do to get their Gross Margins *above* where they had started? His target was that they be high enough to reflect Carlos's productivity gains.

Big Catch had four main options, in roughly the following order of desirability:

First, they could **increase prices**, particularly on the new range. Their best approach would be to freshly calculate the Cost of Goods Sold on the 'Blackwood' range – capturing the increased labor and material costs (including waste). Once that base cost had been established, they could add sufficient margin and establish new prices for the range with the desired Gross Profit. In Carlos and Frank's situation, increasing prices by a small amount was unlikely to have a significant negative effect on sales as the nature of their business was that it did not rely on frequent repeat sales. Only recently they had done some market research and discovered that their pricing was about 10% under what the competition was charging for comparable products. On top of that, I pointed out that in a company like theirs, with a 30-40% Gross Profit Margin, you would need to lose 25% of your total sales to offset the benefit of increasing your prices across the board by 10%. (For a more detailed explanation of the effect of price increases and decreases, and how they might affect your bottom line, visit the Businest® website and sign up for your FREE 14 day trial today.)

Second, they could **reduce costs**, bringing COGS back down to where they needed to be to reflect the Gross Profit they wanted. Their choices here included **increased productivity** – Carlos could do more work on this in the factory – and, possibly, **buying smarter** to reduce the cost of the raw materials. The ability to do the latter would obviously depend on the competitiveness of the timber supply industry.

A third choice was to **reduce value** in their products. They might use less timber, or combine the higher quality timber with a less expensive, lower quality component in some parts of the furniture. Perhaps they could use cheaper, lower quality door hinges and the like. Carlos and Frank didn't want to do this – quality was important to them – but it is always important to consider all the options.

Finally, Carlos and Frank could decide to **stop selling** or reduce the percentage of sales of (or emphasis on) any product – including the new range – which didn't provide their minimum Gross Profit. They could also train the sales team to educate them on the importance of selling more high-margin products.

The order of preference of these choices varies with the specific situation, market dynamics and business (and we'll discuss some of these in the next section).

KEY POINT
It is critical to monitor COGS and Gross Profit regularly and take action to counteract any negative trends. Consistent measurement and monitoring is the only way to avoid nasty surprises at the end of the financial year.

Had Frank been doing this in the same way that Carlos was monitoring the productivity of the factory, he would, at the very least, have spotted the increased timber price as it happened and had the opportunity to legitimately pass this increase on in higher prices. The timber price rise could have been significantly higher and without monitoring in place, Frank's surprise may have been bigger and much more unpleasant.

Keeping it Nice When Things Get Complicated

Pricing for Carlos and Frank was much like their long friendship: comfortable and uncomplicated. They were able to set prices based mainly on their Cost of Goods Sold (COGS) and their target Gross Profit (GP). Their good reputation and the unique, customized nature of their product ensured that, within reason, they could charge what they wanted without the risk of losing sales.

In most businesses, setting prices isn't so simple. Think about the relationship of your invisible employees, Ernest and Penny. Initially it was all about playing games. Penny ran away from Ernest, Ernest (hopefully) caught up and they had a playful tussle. Then Penny ran away again ... and so on. Things changed a bit when they started dating regularly, as we saw in the previous chapter. Suddenly things got more complicated. Expectations were challenged, rules had to be put in place, Ernest had to turn to a bit of psychology for help.

As time goes on, should their relationship become deeper still, what will happen? It will get more complicated still. There will probably be a shared apartment, or a wedding, or both. There'll be joint bank accounts and mortgages. Eventually there might be children – and things will get even more complex.

In most businesses, setting prices is just like this. It becomes a complex interplay between your product and service, your customers, the wider marketplace and the whole economy – not just your COGS. A number of factors, beyond simply cost and margin, come into play.

Let's revisit some of the case studies we've discussed so far and think about the sorts of things these clients had to think about in their pricing decisions.

There was Serge and his café. Serge's menu comprised staple dishes – like coffee and soft drinks, for instance – with a food menu which changed weekly. The prices he set for the staple dishes were determined to largely by the market – in effect by his **competition**. Importantly, an extra 50 cents added to his coffee price could well send many customers to the café two doors up, resulting in not only lost coffee sales but lost food sales as well. On the other hand, a 50 cent drop in price might temporarily attract some new customers but (as we learnt in the opening chapter) could also have a negative effect on Cash Flow.

Setting prices on the food menu was more complicated for Serge. Here he needed to be competitive overall but he also needed to stay in tune with his customers' **expectations**. There would be no point having $8 lunch meals one week, $12 meals the next week and $6 meals the week after. His regular customers – the most valuable of his customers – needed to know what they would pay, if not what they would eat. He could make gradual changes over time, but to a large extent he was stuck with the prices he established in the first place: prices which *positioned* his café in the eyes of his customers. With prices fixed, therefore, in a fairly tight range, and an ever-changing menu, Serge needed to keep a very close eye on the **costs** associated with each meal. He needed his chef to create dishes within a clearly defined budget – a budget that included the cost of preparing meals and the cost of waste (should a particular dish not sell). By using the Businest® tool, Serge learned that the benchmark Gross Profit margin for a café/restaurant was 70 %. This served as a useful guideline to him throughout the coaching process as it highlighted when he needed to adjust his prices or his portions to maintain his desired level of profitability.

For Jason and his domestic electrical business, pricing needed to take into account the two main components of his costs: the **cost of parts**, and the service cost – or **cost of labor**. His advantage was that, most of the time, he was able to review his costs before giving his customer an invoice. The parts price was simple: he simply charged his customers what the wholesaler had charged him, plus a 50% mark-up. He knew that his margin on parts covered the cost of 'consumables' such as wire, screws and so on.

For the **service cost**, Jason had to be more careful. People often undercharge for the services they provide. They either fail to track the time spent on a job and then underestimate how much time they should be billing for, or they charge too low a rate for their time – insufficient to cover 'indirect' time spent on travel, buying supplies, and so on. As Jason charged on a time-basis, his solution was to use a timesheet and a simple chart on which he had pre-calculated charge-out amounts for his time in quarter-hour increments. Included in his rate was sufficient 'slack' to cover the cost of his time spent on those peripheral activities. Over time, Jason learned that the COGS benchmark for his industry was around 38-40%. He was able to track it every single month and could easily adjust his prices upward to cover any changes in underlying costs.

Sam, the photographer, also needed to include a strong service component in her pricing. She spent a lot of time with potential clients working out exactly what they needed before providing a quote. And she spent time on new clients, both face-to-face and on her own, planning her shoots. All of this time needed to be included in her pricing calculations.

But Sam had another, arguably more important, factor to consider in her pricing: her **perceived value.** Just as Penny could change Ernest's early perceptions of her by the way she dressed (and vice versa), Sam was in an industry where she could change her clients' perception of her by how much she charged. As she was aiming to attract clients who cared about quality and didn't mind paying for it, she needed to set her prices at a reasonably high level. To do otherwise would have left clients wondering whether they were really going to get the level of quality they were looking for.

(If you don't believe in perceived value, consider this: bottled water is a huge industry. The price of bottled water is thousands of times higher than that of the virtually equivalent product which comes directly out of your tap. Bottled water is more expensive than petrol – yet the bottled water industry continues to thrive and customers tend to pay the high price without fuss or complaint. Why? Because of its high perceived value.)

Over time, Sam also learned to consider the **complexity** of a job before setting a price. So weddings, for instance, attracted a premium in her pricing calculations. With the emotions involved in wedding photography, these clients (brides and mothers-of-the-bride mainly) were often much fussier than others. The shoots were more complex too, being more dependent on weather, for instance, and involving more on-the-fly decision-making. Sometimes this meant that Sam lost wedding jobs to cheaper competitors, but she knew her costs. Sam once said to me: "If others are prepared to work for lower overall rates by cutting corners or positioning themselves as cheap, good luck to them I say". (Remember, for companies with a 30-40% GP margin, a 10% increase in price means you could lose 25% of your revenue and still end up with the same amount of profit. How would you choose to invest the extra time and profit that would flow from a 10% price increase in your business?)

Carol, in the beauty salon, also charged a higher rate for more complex clients – especially, again, weddings. (Is it any wonder weddings have become so expensive?). But Carol's pricing also varied with the **experience of the staff**. So she was able to offer a lower price to customers willing to have an apprentice cut their hair, while customers wanting Carol herself, or one of her other more-qualified staff, would pay a higher rate.

In retail businesses, other considerations can affect pricing. In some cases, a **recommended price** might largely govern the price charged. This is the way Carol priced her shampoos, for instance. It also guided the way Charlie set prices for his more current range of games and hobbies. However, once Charlie had sorted out his crowded shop and made more sense of it, he increased the prices of some of his older items. He realized that the longer a model kit stayed on the shelf, the greater the **risk of damage, theft or obsolescence**. So he needed to include extra margin in the price of these items to cover the cost of this risk and its associated losses. Byron, in the collectables shop, also included risk of damage in his pricing, but the greater driver of prices in his business was **rarity**. The more hard-to-find an item was, the more he could charge for it. He did need to stay on his guard, however. The advent of the Internet had given his customers much more **price transparency**: they could now compare the prices on rare items all over the world, so there was little scope to overprice – accidentally or otherwise – and get away with it.

Last but not least, we had Craig and Mandy and their commercial plumbing business. In their business, with large-scale projects and even larger developer clients, a serious consideration in addition to price was **payment terms**. The couple's business had over $500,000 owed to it in 'Receivables' at any one time. That's a lot of energy sitting quietly in Ernest's backpack. To offset that amount – to keep 'spending Penny' running until they were paid

– the couple had to borrow an equivalent amount from the bank. Borrowing like this obviously had a cost, and that cost needed to be reflected in their pricing. It meant that if a new client was willing to pay their invoices more quickly (in, say, 10 days rather than 30), they could consider reducing their prices to that client to reflect the equivalent saving in borrowing costs. By contrast, if a client wanted to 'extend terms' and pay in 60 days rather than 30, Craig and Mandy would have to pass on the cost of borrowing money for that period.

So ... setting prices is not necessarily straightforward. There can be many things to consider, of which I have listed only the major ones here. In some ways price-setting makes the increasing complexities of Ernest and Penny's relationship look like a Sunday afternoon stroll. But don't be too discouraged. If you read through the above section again with your own business in mind, you will probably find that of all the factors listed, it's likely that only a few will be relevant to your business.

KEY POINT

Don't treat the setting of prices like a blind date. You should know what your target Gross Profit margin is, and you should know what Costs of Goods Sold (COGS) are associated with everything you sell – both products and services.

And, as stated in the previous section, you should review both your COGS and your Gross Profit regularly in order to stay on top of how well your business is running.

Whip Your Business Into Shape NOW!

Scoring Every Single Time – Proven Strategies to Ensure You Pick Up!

- Take some time to calculate the COGS of every product/service that you sell
- Track the changes in costs (if any) every single month so that you can react quickly
- Calculate the Gross Profit Margin on every product/service that you sell
- Rank your products from highest selling to lowest (in units sold per month)
- On average, what Gross Profit Margin are you earning? (total sales – COGS/total sales)
  - are you happy with it?
  - should it be higher?
- Focus on the Top 20 selling items – do they meet your overall Gross Profit Margin target?
- Increase prices on any or all of your Top 20 sellers
- Make any necessary changes to prices and communicate these to your team and your customers
- Decrease COGS
- Focus on selling more products that have a higher Gross Profit Margin.
- Upsell items with a high Gross Margin (e.g., insurance, training, service contracts, membership programs etc)
- Develop or add new products or services that would give you a higher Gross Profit Margin
- Add a service to your product (like installation or training) that would have a high Gross Profit Margin
- What are your competitors charging? Do you have strong Internet competition?
- Increase the 'perceived value' of your some of your products or services by adding low-cost or no-cost extras
- Vary pricing depending on who is performing the service – charge more for experience
- If adjusting prices, check whether your payment terms need to be amended or adjusted to match

www.businest.com

CHAPTER 5

Is It Really Worth It?

Spot the freeloader in your business...

In This Chapter

How is Your Hard Earned Profit Trapped in Your Business?

Why It's Good to Keep Your Private Affairs Private

Why Growing Your Family Won't Necessarily Make You Happy

"Everyone who lives within their means suffers from a lack of imagination."

Oscar Wilde

Bernie was one of the clients I enjoyed visiting most. She clearly enjoyed life, was extremely optimistic and was passionate about her business. She had started her exporting firm a decade ago and with endless energy had grown the business steadily since then. It now employed a dozen staff and she had links into ten major export markets. Bernie's clients loved her because she was such an enthusiastic advocate for them. On her frequent overseas trips, she was constantly on the lookout for new markets for them. A day would rarely go by without a dozen or so calls back to the office to flag some ideal new opportunity she had just seen for one client or another – complete with contact details to get the discussion going.

I kept in regular contact with Bernie over the years. She had had some coaching from me not long after getting herself set up. She had a good head for business and she understood the benefits of sitting down with an 'outsider' from time-to-time to make sure things were staying on track. A recent topic of conversation had been – surprisingly, I thought – retirement. Bernie enjoyed her work so much I didn't think she would ever want to retire, but she confided to me that she intended to sell the business in five or six years so that she could spend more time traveling for leisure rather than work.

After initially flagging the issue of retirement planning with me, we agreed to spend an afternoon together two weeks later at her house – away from the activity (and the ears) of the business. We would spend the time building a plan to have the business in good shape for sale in five years time.

The first thing I noticed when I pulled up outside Bernie's house was how much it had changed since my last visit two years previously. An upper storey had been added and the outside was freshly painted. In the driveway was a very new BMW four-wheel-drive which I hadn't seen before either.

I commented on these things as Bernie welcomed me inside with her characteristic exuberance.

"Well there have to be some rewards for all my hard work, don't there!" she exclaimed. Feigning a whisper she went on, grinning: "The car's a bit of a dodge really. The depreciation makes me feel less guilty."

"Ah..." I stammered. "So the business bought it then?"

"Yes, of course," she said. "We had built up a good supply of cash so I was able to buy it outright."

All of a sudden I realized that we had more work to do that afternoon than I had thought.

How is Your Hard-Earned Profit Trapped in Your Business?

We talked for a while about Bernie's future plans. Most of it was travel: she had been to enough places by now to have a long list of return journeys she wished to make. After nearly an hour of this I had to pull her up.

"Bernie, we need to move on to the planning or none of this is ever going to happen."

With a sigh she agreed. Our sessions had often been like this. It was definitely her enthusiasm, not her attention to detail, that had driven her company forward over the years. Detail tended to be left to the people she employed.

We talked generalities for a little while: what she thought the business might be worth, what she'd like it to be worth, whether she had any potential buyers in mind – that sort of thing. This meeting wasn't really about number-crunching and it didn't matter at this stage. What was clear was that Bernie wanted to get as much as she could for her business. It was a healthy, profitably business with a proven record and a strong client base. She fully expected that it would be easy to sell for a good price.

"There is one thing that concerns me," I said eventually. "The car."

"How can the car be a problem?" she asked, taken aback.

"Not so much the car itself," I said, "but rather what it represents."

I explained to Bernie that there are essentially three ways to spend cash in a business:

First, cash can be spent on what we might call **production**: on the ongoing costs and expenses associated with doing what it is your business does. This includes everything from stationery to raw materials to telephone bills, from lease payments to rent to wages. These are the bills that keep on coming and that you need Cash Flow to cover. This is the sort of spending represented largely by our 'spending Penny'. Without this sort of spending your business would stop because there would be no one to work, nowhere to work and nothing to work with.

Second, cash can also be spent, when it is available, on what accountants call **Fixed Assets**. As opposed to the regular, ongoing costs of doing your work 'here and now', this spending is spending for the future. It is spending designed to produce income over time. You might buy a machine, for instance, which will produce widgets over its ten-year life. Or a new computer that will make your administrators more efficient over its three-year life. In both cases the spending is happening now but the 'benefit' will be spread over the life of the Asset. A benefit is expected, however. Spending on a Capital Asset is an investment and, like all investments, you will be expecting a return from that spending over time. Think of it as buying new running shoes for Ernest and Penny: money spent now but with an ongoing benefit – at least until the shoes wear out.

Finally, cash can be spent on **Non-Incoming Producing Expenses or Assets**. This is where Bernie's car comes in. As the business paid for the car, it will be included in the list of Assets owned by the business. But unlike its computers or the warehouse, the car will neither produce income of its own, nor indirectly assist with the production of income. This is like feeding Penny up on expensive energy foods, and buying her a nice new running outfit, whilst leaving Ernest in tatty old clothes and without enough to eat.

Sometimes the line between 'income-producing' and 'non-income-producing' Assets can be difficult to distinguish. As a simple example, office pot plants don't produce any income of their own, but they contribute to the 'mood' of employees and customers so could be argued to have an indirect benefit. Extending this argument to a new car for the personal (not business) use of the business owner, however, is a bit of a stretch. In some cases a car or van may be needed in order to conduct day to day business but care must be taken to ensure that you do not buy 'more vehicle' than you absolutely need.

"There is a fundamental difference between the Assets you buy for your business and the Assets you buy for your personal life," I stressed to Bernie.

KEY POINT
All business Assets must produce income.

Why It's Good To Keep Your Private Affairs Private

In our personal lives we buy many things because they give us pleasure. We don't expect a financial return from a new television or a dining setting or a car. In a properly run business, this does not happen.

"But we had the cash," Bernie said after a while. "I don't see how it makes any difference to the business as it hasn't had any effect on the day-to-day running of the business. We still have cash on hand to pay all the bills. And there is no effect on the bottom line."

"That is the dirty little secret of capital spending, Bernie. It can appear as though it is having no effect. But there are at least a three potential effects."

The first 'effect' is that business is all about investment – about making your money grow – and spending business money on Assets that don't facilitate such growth is simply poor business practice. It is no different from the way we invest in other Assets. You wouldn't buy stock or invest in property that has no prospect of kicking up income or a Capital Gain. The same principle applies to the Assets you purchase for your business.

The second, related effect is one that was of particular importance to Bernie as she looked towards selling her business. A key measure of the business's value to potential buyers would be its 'Return on Assets' (ROA). We will explain ROA in more detail and illustrate how to calculate it exactly in Chapter 8. At this point, it is important simply to understand that ROA gives a good indication to a buyer of how good an investment the company might be when compared with other places they could put their money – other companies, or other investments entirely. If Bernie were to continue to add Non-Income Producing Assets to the business – assets which did not increase the Gross Profit – its overall Return on Assets would gradually fall. With that fall would be a corresponding fall in the attractiveness of the business to future buyers.

The final effect of spending cash on Non-Income Producing Assets is that it increases the business's vulnerability by decreasing its Cash Flow. Cash reserves can play an important role in cushioning a business against the unexpected. A sudden drop in sales for reasons outside your control (such as a stockmarket crash or global economic crisis). An unexpected rise in costs. Even the loss of a key employee. The difference between a business which survives these events and one which goes under can be its access to cash reserves. The more the cash reserves of a healthy business are depleted – particularly through buying assets which don't produce any income – the less resilient it becomes.

KEY POINT

There is a very good reason why Richard Branson is rich and you're not. STOP spending your hard earned money on Non-Income Producing Assets! The effect may not be obvious but the impact is negative and significant.

By the end of this long explanation Bernie was looking out her window at the shiny BMW in the driveway. The look was not as enthusiastic as it had been and I noticed that I was getting through. She suddenly brightened, though, and I realized she had one more arrow in her quiver.

"Okay, what about the depreciation then? At least ..." she added with some defiance, "at least I can depreciate the car over time, which reduces the amount of tax we have to pay. Isn't that a form of 'income'?"

"Unfortunately not," I answered. "Depreciation is just an accounting method (a non-cash adjustment) for spreading the cost of an asset out over time. It doesn't change the requirement of the asset to generate income. There are three problems with looking at depreciation as a benefit."

Firstly, while depreciation doesn't affect Gross Profit it does reduce your overall 'Net Profit' and Cash Flow. This is the bottom line profit your accountant – and any potential buyer – will be looking at in judging your business.

Secondly, relating to the tax deduction: there is no benefit to any tax deduction if there is no income to deduct against. While this may not be noticeable with a relatively small Non-Income-Producing Asset, it reinforces the idea that these non-income producing purchases are bad investments in the context of a business.

Thirdly, the tax deduction is effectively a government-funded discount on the price of the car, but all the effects I described earlier still apply to the discounted amount. Bottom line: it is still a bad investment, even if it is made somewhat cheaper by the incentive. You also need to be careful: should the tax department decide to audit your business at some stage, you would need to be able to convince them that the purchase was business-related. They will take a dim view to any dubious Depreciation claim you have made to reduce your taxable income.

KEY POINT

A tax-deduction should only be seen as enhancing the value of an *already* good investment. A tax deduction will *not* turn a bad investment into a good one.

It didn't happen very often, but by the end of this conversation it seemed I had momentarily dampened Bernie's exuberance. But it was only momentary. Aside from boundless energy, Bernie had a healthy intelligence and she was able to see sense in what I was talking about. She just had to come to grips with a different way of operating.

"Perhaps I should save any expensive whims in the future until after I have retired. Once I've sold the business, the money I get will be my own again – it will be what you called 'private money' and I'll be able to do what I like with it. I won't have to be worrying about keeping your Ernest and Penny happy anymore."

Bernie was right. Notwithstanding the need for financial responsibility, her 'private' retirement money could be spent on enjoyment. But there would be more of that money if, in the meantime, her business money were invested in profitable ways, growing the business and improving its value to future buyers.

When I next saw Bernie she was still driving the BMW. She quickly assured me that it no longer belonged to the company – but the company had found a willing buyer!

Why Growing your Family Won't Necessarily Make You Happy

It was an uncomfortable situation. In a somber, timber-lined boardroom I sat with four others at a board table which looked big enough host a game of hockey. Five of us sat in silence. At the top of the table, Martha and Anthony were having a long and private conversation – a conversation the silent majority could not avoid hearing – about the future of their family's business.

"Your father would not have approved of this," said Martha tersely. "He built this business by being careful with money."

Anthony looked to the ceiling and let out a long breath. "But times have changed. We have to move on – have to get modern. It's the right time to do this." He lowered his head and turned his intense gaze to me – which is when things got even more uncomfortable. "Surely you see that, don't you?"

Martha and Anthony's was a fifty-year old printing company. Established by Martha's husband, Helmut, with a single, second-hand press, the business had grown to a healthy size over time. A few years ago Anthony had discovered the original press in a back shed; as a birthday gift to his father he had had it cleaned up and freshly painted. It now held pride of place on display in the company's foyer. These days the printing was performed on three modern offset machines.

Martha had always been heavily involved in the business and after her husband's sudden death two years ago, she had taken on the running of the business. It was no secret that Anthony, their only offspring, would take over eventually. In the meantime, he was in charge of Sales and Marketing, and it was this responsibility that saw him putting pressure on Martha in the boardroom on this day.

From the outset, the business had specialized in long-run print jobs. These days most of their contracts were with government departments which, no matter how tight the budget, always seemed to have money for printing. Full color flyers and information booklets were ordered in the hundreds of thousands. But while this work was lucrative, it was also competitive. Over the past few years, as government purchasing had become smarter, margins had become tighter. Today, a typical job was providing about 20% less Gross Profit than it had been three years previously.

Aside from the obvious impact on the business's profitability, this drop in Gross Profit was making it more difficult for the sales team to achieve their bonuses. Their complaints to Anthony were getting louder. Their message was that the business needed a new machine – a digital printing machine. Such a machine would, they argued, open up new markets, allow them to sell more work and, in turn, get their bonuses back on track.

It was this argument that Anthony had been putting to this mother in the board room, and which he was now looking to me to support. Put simply, his line was this: a digital machine would help the business expand, and as the company had hefty cash reserves and could buy such a machine outright, there was no reason not to do so.

On the surface, this argument had some merit. Clearly this was not another situation like Bernie's as the Asset in question was clearly going to be income-producing. But when properly thought through, the logic had a number of flaws. So when Anthony looked to me over the board table, I had to tell him that, no, I couldn't support his reasoning. It was his mother who was taking the more sensible line.

ᘓ

The underlying problem for Martha and Anthony's business was similar to that faced by Carlos and Frank in Chapter 4: it was a pricing-related problem. Pressure from their customers had seen the printing company's prices fall gradually, while their costs had stayed roughly the same. The result: reduced margin between the price charged and the Cost of Goods Sold (COGS) – that is, reduced Gross Profit (GP).

Where Martha and Anthony's situation differed from Carlos and Frank's was in the proposed solution.

As Anthony's sales team were rewarded, via bonuses, on the basis of the company's Gross Profit as a whole, they – correctly – saw increasing sales as a way to re-establish their bonuses. Anthony and his sales team wanted to achieve this by buying a new digital printing machine. As mentioned earlier, they figured that the new machine would enable the business to market new services, attract new customers, and grow sales from there. Their 'earning Ernest' would be running faster and with the resulting increase in overall Gross Profit, family shopping trips for new televisions and holidays would be just around the corner.

But there was a problem.

What Anthony and his team were not factoring in to their calculations was the fact that buying a new piece of equipment – a new 'Capital Asset' – would change the rules. The new machine would add new costs to the business. It would require new skills, which would come from either costly training or the hiring of additional staff dedicated to that machine. The machine would take the company into unfamiliar markets. Digital was all about short-runs: lots of small orders instead of a small number of large ones. This would stretch the company's existing computer systems, their warehousing capabilities and their administrative skills.

In short, rather than expanding the existing business, adding this new machine would be like adding a whole *new* business alongside the existing one. Rather than making Ernest run faster, the digital machine would effectively introduce a new 'digital' Ernest and Penny to the business. This new couple would run their own race and that race would need to be managed separately. Put another way, adding other people to the family creates additional mouths to feed – and that costs.

And there was another problem the sales team hadn't considered. Digital printing machines were less expensive than the large offset machines the company was used to, and they were easier to run. As a result, there were many more of them out there. Digital machines were appearing in every small photocopy shop, in photo-processing stores, in small print-shops and within existing larger businesses. This digital printing part of the industry was, therefore, highly competitive and so tended to yield lower margins than Martha and Anthony's existing business.

KEY POINT
Adding an Asset is like adding a new business to your existing one. It comes with its own set of costs and targets, largely independent of existing costs and targets, and needs to be considered on its own merits.

I looked directly at Anthony. "The sales targets you'll need to set the sales team on this new machine will be higher than what they have now to achieve the same Gross Profit. And they'll find those sales harder to make and harder to maintain because there will be many more competitors knocking on their customers' doors. In the meantime they'll still have to retain sales on the existing machines or the targets for the new machine will go higher still. What's more, all that will have to happen without adding to the sales team, otherwise the bonuses will need to be spread more thinly. How do you think the team will feel about all that?"

I had been able to make my argument fairly clear and I could see that Anthony understood the main point I was trying to make.

KEY POINT
Adding an income-producing Asset is not an automatic solution to declining Gross Profit Margins.

"So what do you suggest we do then?" he asked.

"Well the obvious solution is one that your sales team may not like, but which they should be more than capable of. That is to sell more work for the existing machines."

The existing machines had ample capacity. One ran only every second day, and overtime was rare. And the factory only ran on one shift. The real problem here was that the sales team had become complacent over time. The government work came in with relatively little sales effort and there hadn't been much time and effort invested in expanding the customer base over the past couple of years. From the perspective of the business as a whole, increasing the throughput of their current machines would increase revenue (speed up Ernest) with very little relative increase in spending (i.e., only a small speed up for Penny). It was clearly the most sensible way of improving their profitability.

Martha spoke up at this point with the final words of before the meeting broke up. "Helmut always believed that bonuses should be a reward for extra effort, not a reward for maintaining the status quo. I would suggest, Anthony, that if your sales team aren't capable of selling more of the work we already do, then you have the wrong sales team."

Neither Anthony nor I could argue with that.

Whip Your Business Into Shape NOW!

Is It Really Worth It? – How Poor Investments Hurt Your Business Without You Even Knowing it.

- Separate all of your Assets into three lists – production, capital and non-income-producing
- Assess the value of the Non-Income Producing Assets – what can be done to remove them from the Balance Sheet and prevent non-income producing purchases in the future?
- Prior to buying any new Asset in your business, calculate the Return on Investment (ROI) that your business will have to generate in order to justify the cost of purchasing it. The value of the Asset (or cost of purchase) should include any and all costs incurred to put the Asset into production – including shipping, installation, finance charges, training, cost of additional staff (if necessary), increases in spending in other areas to compensate (e.g., more admin staff required) and so on.
- ROI = total costs of Fixed Assets / Gross Profit Margin
  - Is the Gross Profit Margin of the sales generated by the new Asset going to be higher or lower than the average in your company right now?
- Assess all commission structures in your business. Is there incentive for your sales team to do what is in the best interest of overall Net Profit?
- Before buying any new Assets, assess the productivity and state of any existing plant and equipment you already have. The easiest way to generate more profit and Cash Flow is to increase the productivity of the Assets that you already own.

www.businest.com

CHAPTER 6

Making the Most of What You've Got

No matter how big or small

In This Chapter

Expand Your Business Without Expanding Costs

The Tipping Point for Time

> *"One does not accumulate but eliminate. It's not daily increase but daily decrease. The height of cultivation always runs to simplicity."*
>
> Bruce Lee

If I remember nothing else about Donna's business, I will always remember the smell. There was a hint of it as I approached the door, but on pushing aside the plastic curtain into the main office it hit me in the face like the blast of heat from an oven. It wasn't an unpleasant smell but the strength of it has stayed with me.

Donna had always loved her food. She'd worked in delicatessens as a teenager, studied food technology at university and got her first job working in the lab, and later in sales, with a major cheese manufacturer. When she and her husband had bought themselves a hobby farm only an hour from the city, Donna decided that the most tasty thing she could do with the fresh milk from their new cow was to make cheese. After a couple of short courses, she found herself spending most weekends producing small batches of camembert and blue cheese – much to the satisfaction of her husband and all their friends.

After coming into an unexpected inheritance (she hardly even knew the uncle who had been so generous to her), Donna left the corporate job she was no longer enjoying and set about making her living with cheese.

By the time I met Donna – and her smells – for the first time, she had a good-sized, temperature-controlled production shed, two small (but *very* pungent) maturing rooms and four full-time staff. She was selling cheeses to good restaurants in the city and through half-a-dozen specialist cheese stores. And she had just won first prize for her camembert at the State cheese show.

Donna's biggest challenge was similar to that of some of my other clients we've met so far – people like Serge and Sam. The business had grown almost despite itself, and certainly more quickly than Donna's knowledge about the ins-and-outs of managing its finer financial points. She was at a point where she wanted to take advantage of her prize win and push the business through another stage of growth. But she didn't want to overstretch and risk losing it all.

"We're happy to put more money into the business, but we want to make sure it is money well spent," she explained. "I've seen too many other businesses in this industry go upmarket in a hurry, then suddenly disappear."

After getting vague answers to a couple of straightforward questions (or so I thought) about how her costs were split between fixed and variable, it was clear we needed to start with the basics.

Expand Your Business Without Expanding Costs

We started with the obligatory introduction to 'earning Ernest' and 'spending Penny'. Here, although Donna obviously didn't know these two personally, I was pleased to see that she did have a grasp of the basic importance of Cash Flow. She had delegated one of her staff to the task of chasing up accounts and this kept Receivables under control. And the nature of the product, which had a relatively short shelf-life, kept pressure on them to sell what they made. This, combined with limited storage capacity for fresh milk, kept inventories down.

It turned out that Donna's food technology and sales experience combined had given her a good understanding of the need to put some science into her pricing. She had carefully calculated the Cost of Goods Sold on all her products, and she was able to charge prices that provided a healthy level of Gross Profit because of the high-end, almost exclusive nature of her product.

Where Donna's understanding broke down was on some of the technicalities of costs and expenses: in particular the difference between 'Fixed Costs' and 'Variable Costs'.

When we talk about 'Costs' in this way – either fixed or variable – we are generally talking about *ongoing* costs which contribute directly or indirectly to the production of the company's products or services.

'Variable Costs' are, as the name suggests, costs which change depending on the amount of work your business does. So in Donna's case, the more cheese she makes, the higher her Variable Costs. The cost of ingredients – milk, for instance – will increase with an increase in production. These are Variable Costs. Packaging is similar, as is the cost of any casual staff, who will usually work more when there is more work to do – hence the cost of their wages is variable.

'Fixed Costs', unsurprisingly, are the opposite. These are those ongoing costs which you will pay regardless of how much product you make. Three of the most common Fixed Costs are rent, wages (of all permanent employees) and advertising (such as a *Yellow Pages* entry).

Imagine Penny jogging along at a steady minimum speed. This speed represents your Fixed Cost spending. Penny will also gather speed at a rate which varies with your production. The more you spend on direct production costs – Variable Costs – the faster Penny will run. If sales, and therefore production, drop, so will this 'variable' component of Penny's speed; the 'fixed' or steady component of her speed will remain the same.

After explaining all this to Donna I paused at this point to let her digest what I'd been saying. I know that this is the sort of stuff that accountants 'get' but many business owners don't. Accountants wonder why their clients are confused because to them it is really simple, while business owners wonder why their accountants spend so much time debating which money should be allocated to which 'box', when it all looks like the same money. The important distinction to understand is that Penny's speed is influenced by two very different types of costs – fixed and variable.

Once I was happy that Donna was with me so far, I ventured on to the next, potentially confusing, point.

"The thing about Fixed Costs is that they are only fixed with respect to the way things are now. As your business changes size, Fixed Costs can change size too."

Take rent, for instance. Imagine an expanding business which leases new, bigger premises. Obviously the business's rental payments would go up, increasing their Fixed Costs. Or say things go bad for a while and the business has to put off a couple of permanent staff. Now their Fixed Costs will drop.

Donna interrupted at this point. "So Fixed Costs can vary, but only with a significant change to the way my business operates. They don't fluctuate on a day-to-day basis with production output, as Variable Costs do."

"That's right," I replied. "And this is where the balance between your Fixed Costs and your Variable Costs becomes relevant as your business grows."

Fixed Costs tend to be a commitment. You can't reduce or stop paying the rent on a whim. You can't sack, or hire, good permanent staff from day to day. You can't drop your *Yellow Pages* advertising once it is in print – it has to be paid for no matter how good or bad a year it is.

Variable Costs are more flexible. If production is halved, you would buy half as many raw materials. You would also reduce the number of casual employees.

"So having more Variable Costs than Fixed Costs is better?" asked Donna. "The more of my costs that are variable, the better placed I'll be to adjust the size of the business to the conditions of the market."

"Not necessarily." I said, "Another way to look at it is this: as you grow, make the best use of the Fixed Costs you have before adding to them." There is a trade off between fixed and Variable Costs. Variable can be more flexible but sometimes you may have to pay a premium for that flexibility (e.g., casual labor may be more expensive per hour than full time employees).

KEY POINT

The aim is to grow your business (output and sales) while keeping Fixed Costs as low as possible as a percentage of sales.

I told Donna about some of the companies I came across back in the days of the dot-com bubble. In those days money was raining down on any business that looked vaguely Internet-related. Start-up companies with little or no income were renting the biggest and best offices in city skyscrapers. They were signing outdoor advertising contracts worth hundreds of thousands of dollars. And their managers were paying themselves enormous salaries.

"Their 'spending Pennys' weren't running, they were sprinting at Olympic speeds. And their 'earning Ernests'? Most of them hadn't even got to the starting line. When things started to teeter and the cash to keep Penny running dried up, these businesses had no way of adjusting their expenditure – it was all Fixed. Their only option was to declare themselves bankrupt and close down."

Compare this situation with one of the dot-com companies that has survived and is now highly profitable: Amazon.com. Amazon started out in a suburban garage with old doors on sawhorses for desks. By keeping their Fixed Costs down as they grew and making best use of their investor's money, they were able to stay in business long enough to start generating profits. They are now a huge company that makes huge profits.

KEY POINT

In order to keep a handle on Fixed Costs, monitor the ratio of Fixed Costs as a percentage of sales (the "Operating Expense Margin) each month. As this percentage decreases, your efficiency and profitability will increase (all other things being equal).

"So what does that mean for someone in my situation?" asked Donna as she looked around her office. "Cheese is a bit different to websites."

Donna was right, of course, but the principle was still relevant to any business.

In our phone conversation Donna had mentioned that she was thinking about setting up a retail store closer to the city as an outlet for her cheese. That, I pointed out, would involve a big step-up in Fixed Costs. Perhaps, I suggested, it might be better to start by creating a 'cellar door' arrangement at her dairy. This would involve a relatively low increase in Fixed Costs initially, with scope to expand gradually over time.

Another alternative for Donna, if she really felt the need to be in a city location, might be partner with an existing outlet, perhaps setting up in a corner of an existing delicatessen. Or she could make arrangements with her existing retail outlets to feature her products on a rotating basis. (This is the same sort of thinking that owners of office-based businesses can use:

starting out with a serviced office, a shared office or a home-based office keeps Fixed Costs down while opening up new markets and opportunities.)

Selling product online is another way many businesses are increasing their 'reach' without increasing their Fixed Costs. Even perishable foods like cheese are being sold this way.

Many manufacturing businesses can get more production out of their existing space simply by tidying up, rearranging the layout of machines and planning more cleverly (to reduce work in progress). Factories and warehouses tend to be like homes: the amount of 'stuff' in them expands to fill the space available. Higher efficiency is nearly always there if you look hard enough.

Making better use of time is another way to increase production with minimal impact on Fixed Costs. Donna had the potential to do this already. Her dairy operated just one eight-hour shift, five days per week. Her options included doing some production on weekends, or running for twelve hours a day during the week, or even adding an evening shift. All of these options would have their challenges, and she may have needed to build some extra maturing space, but all would have been less expensive – and more flexible – than, say, duplicating the factory space and machinery that she already had.

There are many more options, and these would vary with each situation, but the key point is this:

KEY POINT

The best way to keep Fixed Costs low is to make maximum use of the Fixed Costs you already have. Avoid increasing Fixed Costs in order to look bigger than you really are. You might never get there!

As Donna started to recognize all her options for growth without excessively increasing Fixed Costs, she put more extravagant options out of her mind and started focusing on the smaller, more practical ideas. A 'cellar door' was her preferred option. She pointed out to me that an added benefit of this option was that it would make better use of her existing premises in the 'off season' for cheese-making. In mid winter, when cows are typically producing low quantities of milk of a lower quality, it was not cost-effective to produce cheese. Donna and her staff – and the factory – had been taking three weeks off in this time, but adding a shop to the factory would "level things out".

As we ended our conversation, Donna did have one question for me. "When we talk about maximizing Variable Costs for flexibility, does that mean I should be using mostly casual staff rather then permanent staff?"

It was a good question. The answer was that, as with most things like this, there is some balance needed. There are advantages and disadvantages to the use of casual staff over permanents. Casual employees can cost you more than you think. You might spend a lot of time training casuals unless you can bed down a regular crew. And sometimes their loyalty is not as strong as a permanent employee's because – put bluntly – your loyalty to them is not as strong either. On the other hand, it is more difficult to vary the hours of permanent staff and the inherent level of commitment is higher. There is no single answer here. Each business needs to find its own level, keeping the need for balance in mind.

The Tipping Point for Time
(aka The Magic Moment When Time Starts to Work For You Not Against You)

We can take the concept of getting most out of what you already have – your 'Fixed Costs' – a step further by looking at whether the use of your own, individual time is cost-effective. In Chapter 5, about Assets and ROI, I made the point that, in business, every Asset should be income-producing. The same applies to the way you should look at your time when that time is being spent in your business.

To demonstrate what I mean, let me tell you about two other clients of mine: Sunil, a mortgage broker, and Tracy, a graphic artist.

Sunil's was the classic story of the early 2000s. Having been offered a healthy redundancy from his job as a project manager in a telecommunications company, he had decided to invest his payout in a mortgage-broking franchise. His timing was spot-on. He managed to get in as the housing price boom was really picking up pace and public awareness of broking services was similarly growing.

Sunil had started working from home but in a short time got to the point that to really run his business effectively, and to take full advantage of the high level of interest in his industry, he was going to need a small shopfront. He found the perfect spot: a vacancy came up in a small strip of shops on one of the main roads only ten minutes from his house. There were two real estate agents in the group of stores, and the location was accessible to both an established but burgeoning suburb and some of the new estates popping up a little further out. Within a few weeks his office was up and running and his business was soon operating on a new level.

Then Sunil met his first major challenge. Caught in the typically difficult period between being a busy one-person business or a not-busy-enough for two-people business, he asked me to help him work out which way to go. By relying wholly on himself to do all the work, he felt he was badly limiting his growth. But he wasn't confident that he could afford to take on an extra staff member just yet.

A few days after he had called me, I visited Sunil in his office. It certainly looked the part: prominent signage and the strong colors of his well-known brand, and a small but thoroughly professional-looking office. When I arrived Sunil was on the phone so I started my investigation immediately by subtly listening in to his conversation. It was a potential client trying to set up an appointment at their home. No sooner had that call finished than the phone range again; Sunil excused himself and spent a few minutes making another appointment.

Eventually things went quiet for long enough that Sunil was able to have a chat to me. We talked through where he had been and how he was feeling about the business – which was mainly positive. "If only I had a bit more time," was one comment. He showed me the quite detailed systems that the franchisor had supplied him. There were spreadsheets, forms and brochures which took both Sunil and potential applicants step-by-step through the process of shopping for the ideal loan and thereafter making the application. There was a bit of paperwork involved – which is the nature of mortgages – but overall the systems looked pretty good. I couldn't see a lot of time savings for Sunil in changing any of them.

My mind returned to the overheard phone conversations. I had a hunch about where Sunil might find some more time without, for the time being, taking on an assistant.

"Could we have a look at your diary together?" I asked.

Sunil opened it up to the current week. He walked me through the appointments, telling me what each client was looking for. It was a busy diary, but the thing that struck me most was that there were gaps of at least an hour between each appointment. There was probably 16 hours – nearly two days work – left open in this way – which was having a large negative impact his 'profit-per-hour'. When I asked about this, Sunil explained that it was travel time.

"Not every appointment is an hour away from the next, but I have to allow an hour in case a meeting goes over time, or for heavy traffic, and so on. I learnt that lesson when I was working from home."

"But now that you have this office, don't some people come to you? Surely that would reduce your travel time?"

"Not really," he replied. "People still like me to go to them, and I just have to fit them in when I can."

After pressing Sunil on this for a little while, his problem – or rather opportunity – became clear. Sunil had only two major Fixed Costs: his own salary, and his rent. He wasn't making the best use he could of either. Essentially Sunil had to find a way to spend more of his hours on work that contributed to his income, that is, talking to clients and processing their applications. He had to spend less time in the car.

We tossed around a few ideas. As a trial, we agreed that he would spend two days a week in his shop. He would advertise this fact to new enquirers, giving them the chance of an earlier appointment if they were willing to come to the store. He would continue to spend his other days on the road, making house calls, as this was clearly what most clients wanted. But he would group these appointments geographically, allowing him to schedule 30 minutes, rather than an hour, between each. Instead of giving his clients free reign over his diary, he would give them a couple of options for appointment times – plus the 'in-store' option.

When I spoke to Sunil two weeks after this meeting, he sounded very enthusiastic. The measures he had introduced had had a big effect: he was now fitting ten extra clients in each week. He had started measuring his 'profit per hour' and seen the number increase by over 20%. As a bonus, spending the two full days in the office had allowed him to get more efficient at processing applications and he was spending less time working at home.

Two months later he had taken the step of looking for an assistant, but he was now doing so with much higher confidence that the business could feed this extra 'mouth'.

KEY POINT

As a business owner or manager, your own time is one of your most valuable Fixed Costs. Make sure you are getting the most out of it by spending as much time as possible on income-generating work.

Tracy was a client of mine who ran a home-based graphic design business. She was well set up: she had a studio/office separate from her house, so she was able to draw a clean line between work and home without the added expense of renting an office. Her business never required clients to come to her: she would either go to them or, increasingly, she would take briefs over the phone and by email, without the need for a face-to-face meeting at all. In short, she was quite happy in her home office and had no intentions of getting so big that she would have to move out.

Tracy's problem was that she was having trouble converting her budget into reality. She had invested some time calculating what she wanted to earn, how much work she could do and, therefore, what rates she needed to charge. And while she had no trouble winning work at those rates, she always seemed to be falling short of her budget.

When I called on Tracy to help her find out where the problem lay, I asked if I could see her time-sheets or records. Her underlying problem exposed itself straight away when she answered: "I don't have any".

It turned out that while Tracy charged her provided her clients with quotations based on her hourly rate, she was not tracking how many hours she was actually spending on each job. Being a conscientious person, she knew that she was spending more time on most jobs than she should have been, but she had no idea how long. I knew. Well, I didn't know precisely, but I did know from previous experience that if she wasn't tracking her time, she was spending a lot more time on her jobs that she perceived.

KEY POINT

Our perceptions often mislead, especially when it comes to Time. The amount of time we spend on a task or project is nearly always longer than we think it is.

This was the time to tell Tracy about my experiences as a lawyer. In my early days I had practiced law with a very large firm in Canada. It had been a great introduction to time-keeping because time-keeping is one thing lawyers do extremely well!

As a junior lawyer, every minute of every day had to be accounted for. To be precise, every six minutes. On my desk sat a time sheet which broke each day into six-minute increments. Throughout the day, I had to record which client and case I was working on in every one of those intervals. So if I was interrupted by a phone call from a client, the time on that call was attributed to them. After the call I would return to recording time against the case I had been working on beforehand.

These time sheets were collated daily and recorded by our assistants in the practice's computer system. When it came time to bill a client, all the time recorded against that client would be added together and the invoice raised accordingly.

There is no space for misperceptions of time in a law firm.

I suggested to Tracy that she might do something similar. She might not quite go to the extent of recording every six-minute interval, but she might record quarter-hour or half-hour intervals. Tracy could then use these records, after a while, to better inform her quotes – allowing her to quote more realistically. And on more open-ended jobs, she could negotiate with her client simply to charge them for time, on the basis that, like a law firm, she would provide detailed time records with each invoice.

Tracy ended up using a small computer program to help her automate the allocation of her time to her jobs (there are many of these programs available now, or you may choose to use a simple spreadsheet). She was immediately surprised by how much time in her day was being lost to distractions like social networking (she had become a keen Twitter and Facebook user), so before changing anything from her clients' point of view she found that the time records made her more disciplined about her time usage. She was also, as I had expected, 'giving away' about 20% of her time by putting extra uncharged hours into her jobs. Her newfound clarity helped her improve this situation by charging accordingly. Surprisingly, she found that her clients hardly noticed her higher charges, such was the quality of her work.

KEY POINT

When the value of work is calculated on a time basis, the time used to do that work must be carefully recorded and billed to the customer. Recording your time will also reveal sources of 'lost' time such as social networking distractions and personal telephone calls.

Whip Your Business Into Shape NOW!

Making The Most of What You've Got – Here are the Quickest Ways to Expand Your Business Without Expanding Your Fixed Costs!

- Run a Profit and Loss (Income) Statement using your accounting package. If you don't have one, keep track of all revenues and expenses in a spreadsheet which is updated each week at a minimum.
- Examine each of the costs on your Profit and Loss – familiarize yourself with those that are fixed and those that are variable
    - As a general guideline, Variable Costs will appear above your Gross Profit line (ie, they are part of COGS)
    - All costs below Gross Profit should be fixed in nature
    - Reclassify any expenses which are not in the right category
- Track your Operating Expense Margin each month (this is just a simple percentage of your Fixed Costs divided by your Total Sales). As this number decreases, it is an indication that your business is running more efficiently – the Fixed Costs are producing more income. (Businest® will keep track of this KPI and let you know when it starts to increase and requires your attention.)
- Before you expand your business into another area, product, market etc, think of all the possible alternatives which would allow you to do this without increasing your Fixed Costs.
- Assess how you could re-arrange your business to make better use of existing space, capacity and resources.
- For one week, keep track of everything you do in half-hour blocks or increments. The easiest way to do this is to use a simple spreadsheet. At the end of the week, total all of your income generating time and your non-income generating time. This will give you a rough idea of how productive you are.
- You may also want to measure how much time you spend as a percentage each week working ON rather than just IN your business.

Working ON your business includes time that you spend in business planning, customer and marketing strategy, reviewing KPIs and progress, training, reading and growing your own knowledge base, team building etc. The more time you spend ON your business, the more successful you will become.

- Assess how your business could benefit from grouping important tasks together to minimize any wasted or non-productive time.
- Honestly assess how much time you waste every day checking emails, sitting on the telephone or messing around on Twitter and Facebook. Make a plan to only check emails and return calls (unless they are an emergency) between certain specified hours in the day. Block these times out in your diary and evaluate your progress and time savings.
- If you charge out by the hour, start recording your (and any employees') time spent on jobs in 15-minute increments. Assess the total of hours worked versus the number billed out to each client. You should also measure the productivity of each employee in terms of hours worked versus hours billed and collected.

www.businest.com

CHAPTER 7

Stop Playing Around: It's Time to Commit

If ignorance equals bliss, then you'll be broke

In This Chapter

"There is no difference between a pessimist who says 'Oh, it's hopeless, so don't bother doing anything,' and an optimist who says, 'don't bother doing anything, it's going to turn out fine anyway.' Either way, nothing happens."

Yvon Chouinard

Walking into Todd's showroom was like walking into a department store. Scanning the rows and rows of household products I was left wondering who on earth used all these things? There were kitchen gadgets with obscure shapes and even more obscure purposes. Bathroom accessories with enough color options to make a paint company proud. Storage solutions for everything from a few grams of ground spice to a wardrobe full of clothes. More astonishing was the fact that every time I visited Todd, the showroom range seemed to have changed. Clearly there were a lot of people in the world spending a lot of time designing new 'things'.

Todd's office and showroom oozed success. It was clean, shiny and modern. A new customer would be left in no doubt that they were dealing with a professional organization. The problem was that, behind the scenes, things weren't so polished.

Todd had been a client of mine for a few years. His business had grown at a good rate – a rate that Todd felt comfortable with and which I, as an observer, also felt was generally under control. As an importer and wholesale distributor of an always expanding, always changing range of homewares, Todd's business had surfed a surging consumer economy for a good six or seven years. All of which meant Todd was generally a happy person: a rare business owner without a lot of concerns about the immediate future.

There was a day more recently, however, when Todd met me with a more worried expression.

"How is it possible," he asked almost before I had put my bag down, "that we can suddenly be struggling to break-even? The month before last we came to the end of the month and things were tighter than I thought, but I figured it was a one off. Last month, which I got the figures for yesterday, we actually fell just behind. We haven't done that for years – if ever."

Is Not Knowing Your Break-even Keeping You Poor?

Now before I continue with this story, let's define what is meant by Break-even. We say a company breaks even for a period (usually a month) when its sales revenue catches up to its costs. Specifically, accountants talk about Break-even as the point where 'Fixed Costs' (rent, salaries, etc – see the last chapter) have been matched by 'Gross Profit Margin' (Sales revenue minus COGS).

A more simple way to think about Break-even is in terms of 'earning Ernest' and 'spending Penny'. Imagine that Ernest and Penny play their chasing game every month. At the start of the month, Penny is given a head-start – a handicap – because there is some spending (the Fixed Costs) that will happen even if the business produces nothing. When the month starts, Penny starts running as money is spent on the costs of producing new goods or services. Ernest starts running too, as new sales are made. Assuming that Ernest is running faster than Penny (that there is some Gross Profit), Ernest will slowly catch up to Penny. The point at which Ernest catches up to Penny – when earnings catch spending – is the 'Break-even Point'.

So let's return to Todd's business. Todd had, historically, reached the end of each month having easily broken-even. His Ernest usually caught up to and passed his Penny well before the end of the month. But recently things had changed. Ernest seemed to be struggling. Two months ago he had just caught up to Penny by the end of the month. In the most recent month, he had fallen short of catching up before a new month started and Penny was given a new head-start.

I asked Todd the same question I ask all my clients when they find themselves having trouble breaking-even: "How are you measuring Break-even?"

"I get a rough idea on the last day of the month by looking at how many invoices have been raised and the total sales figure. Over the years, on average, if we've raised 400 invoices at an average of $2,500 each, things work out okay. Then, a few days later, the accountants give me the end-of-month financial statements which give me the full picture.

"And that's when I'm getting surprises," Todd went on. "The rule-of-thumb '400 invoices at $2,500' has been okay. But when the final numbers come in, we are, as I said, either square with or just behind Break-even. I don't like these sorts of surprises."

Todd's situation was becoming more clear. He had, in fact, two main problems. The first was that something had changed which was causing his profitability to fall. The other was that he had no idea there was a problem, or how big it was, until after the end of the month. The old saying about shutting the gate after the horse has bolted had never been truer. In order to keep things clean I decided to work with Todd on the two problems separately.

First Impressions Can be Deceiving

Over the years Todd and I had shared various consultations covering many of the issues in this book. We had worked hard on getting his inventory management under control – not an easy thing to do in a business like his. But he had employed some smart people in this area and these days he was right on top of any aging stock and the like. We had also worked on his Receivables and Payables, and on monitoring Cash Flow. Again, as the business had grown – with more customers of a wider range of types (from large department stores to small discount stores) – these had become more of a challenge. Careful management and, again, the identification of good staff, had seen these brought under control too. Another area we had worked on was Fixed Costs. As a fast growing business, Todd had been similar to Donna (in Chapter 6) in being at risk of raising his Fixed

Costs more quickly than the business could absorb. But he understood the principles we discussed and had managed this well also.

With all that behind us, I was able to ask a few quick questions to try and narrow down the problem of the disappearing profitability. In particular, had his Fixed Costs changed significantly in the last couple of months? This would make his Break-even point higher.

> **KEY POINT**
> **An increase in Fixed Costs, all else being equal, will raise the Break-even point: more sales will be needed to offset the higher Fixed Costs, before Sales start contributing to Profit.**

"No. I looked at that when the problem arose, but Fixed Costs have been pretty stable. That's one of the reasons I'm scratching my head: if Fixed Costs are unchanged, and our sales revenue is also more-or-less the same, how can Break-even be different?"

"The answer," I replied, "has to be in the one part of the equation that you haven't mentioned: Gross Profit, or Gross Profit Margin. Your margin must have fallen, raising the value of sales needed to Break-even."

"But how can that be an issue? We've talked often enough about pricing. You know that we work hard to make sure our prices are high enough to cover our costs and to meet our target margin overall. And the mix never seems to change ..."

Todd paused and looked out the window. "... or does it? Perhaps the mix has changed. That could be it." And without even looking to me for confirmation, he was on the phone to his financial accountant, requesting a sales breakdown for the past three months by Gross Margin.

What Todd had realized – and it was proven by the figures which landed on his desk soon afterwards – was that the average margin of his total sales had dropped.

What does that mean in English? Recall Chapter 4, when Carlos and Frank discovered that with their new range of furniture, the costs (COGS) had gone up by more than the increased prices they were charging: the gap between those two, their Gross Margin, had become smaller. Ernest was running faster, but Penny was running faster still.

The same thing was happening in Todd's business, though the nuts-and-bolts were a little different. With such a large range of products, targeted at different stores and different types of customers, some of his products were able to sell at high Gross Margins (up to 80%) while at the 'discount store' end, there were products selling for only 20% Gross Margin. To keep this simple, let's imagine that his sales representatives were making half their sales at the 'top end', the 80% end, with the other half at the 20% end. The average Gross Margin would, therefore, be 50%. This figure had remained fairly steady for two years, so Todd had got out of the habit of checking for any change in it.

Recently, it turned out, there had been a change. There had been a dip in consumer confidence and Todd's people were finding it harder to sell the more expensive products. In their place, the cheaper, lower margin products were selling better than ever. Overall, Todd's total sales figures were more or less unchanged ... but the average margin on those sales had dropped to 40% in one month and 35% in the next. Now they needed to sell more in order to make the same Gross Profit Margin and to reach their Break-even point – but they weren't doing that.

KEY POINT

A fall in Gross Margin increases the Break-even point: more sales are needed in order to offset Fixed Costs. Discounting to increase sales will not achieve the desired result because it decreases the Gross Margin further still.

"That end-of-month promotion," I had to point out, "was probably the cause of the extra drop in margin last month. Discounting always brings the Gross Margin down – as I've told you many times before. What's more, end-of-month spikes in sales have many additional hidden costs as your logistics people, in particular, scramble to send a high number of orders out in a short time. Mistakes are made and people get stressed and customers get annoyed. And then there's the rework."

"Now you sound like my mother," Todd laughingly replied. "But I get the message. If we are going to get things back on track, we need to change our targets. We either need to sell more at the current Gross Margin, or we have to get the margins and profitability back up by restoring sales of our more expensive products."

"That's right. You have to do all that – and you have to do something else too, perhaps even more important: you have to start tracking your performance against Break-even much more closely."

When You're Ready to Get Serious…

Imagine you are playing an important game of tennis. It's the club final and you are the favorite to win. There is a big crowd watching and as the game progresses, everything seems to be going to plan. You're playing well and you're winning points. Victory can't be far away. There is only one problem: there is no scoreboard, and the umpire is keeping the score to herself. So no one except the umpire knows what's really going on.

Nevertheless, you plough on and, despite being in the dark about the score, you feel positive that eventually the umpire will declare you the winner. You are so confident that you can't help but relax just a little. You start enjoying the party-like atmosphere.

Then a shock! Out of the blue, the umpire declares that it is match-point ... to your opponent! You can't believe it. You go back to the baseline, determined, and set yourself up for this big point. But to no avail. It's too late to get your mind back into gear and you hit the return wide. The game is over, the final is lost. If only you'd been able to track the score during the game. At least you would have been able to fight back a little bit earlier.

Every day, hundreds of businesses, big and small, operate as though they are playing a game of scoreboard-less tennis. It is exactly what Todd was doing. Every month he would run on feelings for most of the month – no more than a perception about how well the business was traveling. A day or two before the month ended, he would look to the 'umpire' – his accountant – who would give him the 'score' – his sales figures. And most times, until two months ago, his perceptions had proved fairly accurate. The problem was that when things changed – when his 'opponent' started to get on top – he didn't see it coming.

"There are many things you need to measure in your business," I counseled, "but one of the most important to measure frequently is your Break-even. It is to your business what the main scoreboard is at a sporting contest. And when I say 'frequently', I don't mean weekly or even every few days. I mean *daily*."

KEY POINT

Daily tracking of Break-even is essential to keeping control of your business. Daily-tracking means you see small changes as they happen and can react to them. It reduces nasty surprises.

At this point Todd – like many people – was a bit confused. He could understand the need to monitor his measurement frequently, but he wasn't sure what to measure. "But the 'Break-even point' is just that – a point. We've either broken-even or we haven't."

"That's true. But there are a number of ways you can monitor your progress towards that line, or towards any target you wish to aim for. And the keyword there is 'target'. Let's set this up from the beginning."

I asked Todd what he was aiming for each month.

"Well, to break-even, I guess. That's what we're talking about now, isn't it?"

"But breaking-even isn't enough, is it? To break-even just means your revenue has caught up to your costs. If you were to break-even, but only break-even, every month you wouldn't actually be making a profit, would you?"

Todd agreed. Think in terms of Ernest and Penny: Imagine Ernest catching up to Penny month after month, and, having caught up, jogging alongside her, but without any talking, any holding hands, any interaction at all. Same thing, every month. There wouldn't be a lot of relationship development would there? What's needed is commitment. Ernest needs to run *past* Penny and urge her to catch up. They need to get to know each other, interact with each other, play with each other. They need to build their relationship. We might call the business equivalent of this relationship development: 'building a profit'.

After a few moments thought, Todd realized where I was going with all this. "What you are suggesting, I think, is that we need to be aiming for something more than Break-even. We need to be aiming for a healthy profit figure."

"You got it. You start the year with a budget and part of that budget is a profit figure – the profit you want to make. Dividing that annual figure by twelve, you come to a monthly profit target. If you are for real about achieving that figure – if you are committed to it – that should be your real Break-even target. I call it 'Break-even plus Profit'."

KEY POINT

Aiming for Break-even only is like having a relationship without any commitment. 'Break-even plus Profit' is a more meaningful, sustainable and committed target.

One good thing about dealing with Todd was his quick understanding. He immediately saw that aiming for 'Break-even plus profit' instead of just 'Break-even' would change his targets. "So where our rule of thumb has been '400 invoices at $2,500', it would need to be higher. Either more invoices or higher average value. That makes sense – but it is only a change in the target. It doesn't change the situation I find myself in now. Changing the target won't remove the surprises."

He was right. Changing the target to 'Break-even plus Profit' is only the first step. The next step is to break the target down into smaller increments: into monthly, weekly and daily targets.

So, in Todd's case, instead of aiming for, say, '600 invoices at $2,500' over the month, he might aim for 30 invoices per trading day. (I'm assuming 20 trading days per month.) But he could go further. He could allocate a daily target per sales representative. Todd has five salespeople, so that would be six invoices each per day.

You can vary the daily target depending on what suits your business. You might go for a dollar sales figure per day, or a number of invoice lines. You might, if you have the capability in your reporting systems, target a daily Gross Profit figure.

"Having established a daily target for 'Break-even plus Profit', you can look at both Break-even and 'Break-even plus Profit' another way – and this can be particularly useful," I told Todd. "Determine how many days' sales are needed to reach the Break-even point. Say it takes 14 trading days to reach that point – assuming you operate at your target rate of 30 invoices per day. 14 days becomes a monthly checkpoint. Break-even by that point and you can relax a little in the knowledge that 'everything from now on is pure profit'. You can monitor progress – every day – towards that checkpoint. No more surprises. If you fall behind, you can give the salespeople a rev-up to correct things. If you get ahead, you might reassess your goals for the month."

When you operate towards a mid-month Break-even target, you are like the tennis player who is adjusting his play to the progress of the game. Fall behind, and you might lift the aggression. Get ahead and you might play a little more defensively. Either way you are being *proactive* in the way you run your business, on a daily basis, as opposed to letting things happen and allowing circumstances to take control.

KEY POINT

Establishing which day of the month you should Break-even, and then tracking progress up to and beyond that day, is a simple way to keep close contact with your business's progress.

"I guess we could go one step further again," Todd said, "and work out what day we will meet our 'Break-even plus Profit' goal. All being well, we would meet that goal on the last day of the month. In a good month we might meet it on, say, trading day 17 – giving us three days of 'bonus' trading. In a not-so-good month, we might look like meeting that goal on trading day 23 – in other words missing the target."

"Yes, but either way you will know *ahead* of time how things are going and be able to take appropriate action to either catch up, or deal with the shortfall. No more surprises."

Break-even is relevant even in the context of a Non-Profit

I worked once with a childcare centre – a community-based childcare centre – which was a Non-profit organization. Non-profit organizations have their own set of complications when it comes to the notion of breaking-even. The charter of a non-profit organization is that they, not surprisingly, aren't allowed to make a Profit. While this strictly means that no Profit can be paid out to anyone – and therefore small Profits if made need to retained – the onus was on the management team to keep any surpluses to a minimum. As a community-based centre their aim was to keep fees as low as possible by matching them to costs.

What did this mean for Break-even? Well it was very simple. The child-care centre couldn't make a loss; it needed to Break-even – just – by the end of each month. They wanted their Ernest to just catch up to – but not pass – their Penny every month.

Now this may seem like a simple goal, but in practice it can be quite difficult to achieve. Costs always vary slightly, even with the best laid plans. In childcare there is always an obligation to have, say, one staff member for every five children. That means that if you have six children, you are obliged to have another staff member, which raises the average cost of staffing per child. On the 'sales' side – in this case represented by attendances – things can also change quickly without a lot of notice. A sudden cold snap might see more parents keeping their children at home, and hence a drop in revenue.

In this organization it was imperative that Break-even performance was monitored regularly. As with Todd, I encouraged use of daily tracking. By knowing where they stood against their Break-even target, the staff could make adjustments to their staffing arrangements, or even to their catering arrangements, to fine-tune their performance as they went along. This ensured, for instance, that they didn't reach the last week of the month with either a glut of food, or a shortage of food – nor a glut or shortfall of cash.

I could always rely on Todd to take action after one of our discussions. He called me a week later to say he had worked with the accountants to convert the budget figures into daily 'Break-even' and 'Break-even plus profit' targets based on sales figures. He had dispensed with the 'number of invoices' measure because, in his case, the new daily targets made this redundant. He had set up a very simple chart on a whiteboard in the staff meeting room showing 'Target Break-even Day' and 'Target Break-even plus Profit day', and the current values of both those numbers based on sales so far in the month. (For good measure, Todd had shared the Ernest and Penny story with his staff and, with the numbers, he had drawn Ernest catching up to Penny on 'Break-even' day and Ernest running ahead of Penny on 'Break-even plus Profit' day.)

Todd mentioned how the simplicity of these measures was getting good feedback from the staff. They appreciated that on a daily basis they could see how the business was going and already felt that they were making some attempt to adjust their efforts when it looked like one of the target days might not be met.

Some time later he called me again. This time he was on an overseas holiday. He wanted to tell me that the target days numbers had become so reliable that instead of having whole spreadsheets emailed to him every few days, he was simply having the accountants send him a text message showing 'current days to Break-even plus Profit'. This one number, he said, was enough to keep him happily in touch while traveling.

Separately, Todd had also worked with the accountants to improve their tracking of Gross Margin through the month. They didn't confuse the daily targets by trying to incorporate margin into those targets. What they did do was review, on a weekly basis, the average Gross Margin. This gave them time during the month to take corrective action if things got out of hand. He had removed another potential source of surprises.

It came as no surprise to me that within a few months, Todd's business was operating at a higher level of productivity. And the worried expression had left Todd's face.

Whip Your Business Into Shape NOW!

STOP Playing Around – Action Steps You Need to Take if You Are Serious About Your Business!

- Calculate your Break-even – it's a simple formula of total Fixed Costs divided by your Gross Profit Margin
- Now calculate your 'Break-even with Profit' – simply add your desired Profit figure to your total Fixed Costs and divide that by your Gross Profit Margin
- Determine what is the best way to break your Break-even with Profit number for the month into smaller bite size chunks that you can share with the team in the form of sales targets
    - Break the figure down into daily or hourly sales targets
    - Break the figure down into number of transactions per day (number of sales x average sale amount)
    - Try calculating the trading day of the month that you break even on – i.e., is it the 20th or the 30th day of the month?
- Put a system in place to monitor Break-even and the important KPIs in your business throughout the month (like average $ sale, total Fixed Costs, Gross Profit Margin etc) to avoid nasty surprises
- Remember, your KPIs will change as your business changes – it is important to monitor them regularly and take action to maintain and enhance your profitability
- Review your targets and sales incentives to ensure that your team is focused and motivated to sell products or services which enhance your Gross Profit Margin (not decrease it)
- Adjust your promotional offers to add value and upsell rather than discount
- Look for ways to smooth out sales over the month and avoid putting pressure on your administration and fulfillment channels at the end of the month (eg, minimize overtime to keep up with end of month sales rushes to meet targets)
- Take up the FREE 14 day trial of Businest® – why calculate all of this manually when our online proprietary software will automatically calculate your Break-even (with and without Profit) each month and break it down into easy to understand KPIs that you can share with your team?

CHAPTER 8

Yours or Mine?

Finding the right balance can by risky business

In This Chapter

Chapter 8 - Yours or Mine?

"Give me a lever long enough and I could move the world."

Archimedes

It seemed too good to be true and, in the end, it was.

For years, Eric and Helen had dreamed of spending their retirement running their own bookstore. Since meeting in an antique bookshop all those years ago, both books and bookstores had always been their strongest shared passion. They had no desire to travel anymore, and no desire to sit around the house either. A bookstore would do them nicely.

In their minds, though, this was still a few years away. Eric had it all worked out. He'd worked out what their superannuation payouts would be if they retired at 62. He'd calculated that by investing a lump sum in an established shop, they would be able to buy a small, existing store in an inner suburb and, given a reasonable turnover, they would be able to get by on the profits from that store, topped up if necessary by regular income from their remaining investments.

Their plans changed after they visited a franchising exhibition. One of the franchisors displaying their wares was a bookshop chain. On the wall of the display were pictures of stores which were currently looking for buyers – established franchises for sale. One of those on the wall was the outlet in Eric and Helen's local shopping centre, a store they had spent countless hours browsing in over the years.

"This store is for sale now?" Eric directed his question to the smartly presented man sitting at the nearby desk.

"Certainly is," he replied. "The owners finalized their arrangements with us only last week and so we now have the pleasure of helping them to sell what is a very strong little business."

At this point, when Eric recounts the story, things get a bit blurry. He freely admits that emotions kicked in. The couple knew that this was a once in a lifetime chance to buy a store they already regarded as 'theirs'. Roughly what happened next is that Eric and Helen immediately sat down with Travis, the franchisor representative, to learn what they would have to do to buy the franchise themselves. In many respects Travis's job was easy: Eric and Helen had already decided what they were going to do. Travis just had to help them find a way to buy the franchise five years earlier than they had planned, and without access, yet, to the superannuation savings that they had been counting on.

Both Helen and Eric describe Travis as having been incredibly helpful. He had explained to them that there are always two ways to the money for a business: you can use your own capital, or you can borrow someone else's. The great advantage, he had explained, of borrowing money is that you can leverage your efforts: you can either invest more money and thereby generate greater returns, or – as in the case of Eric and Helen – you can use borrowed money to take advantage now of an opportunity which may never be there again. Travis pointed out that after so many years of working in good jobs and spending responsibly, Eric and Helen were in the perfect position to borrow. They would easily be able to re-mortgage their house – they could probably get access to a much bigger loan than they had had originally. And if they needed to top things up with a personal loan or the like, Travis was sure that their responsible financial history would hold them in good stead. What's more, any interest they paid on a business loan would be tax deductible.

Helen told me that Travis had been very thorough on their behalf. He had cautioned them against making the purchase before they had a good understanding of what they were buying. He had attained the financial statements of the business and had walked through them carefully, making sure that Eric and Helen both understood what sort of return they could expect on their investment, based on what the current owners were achieving, what the rent and other outgoings would be, and what the components of the purchase, including the existing Inventory, would be.

Things gathered pace almost immediately after that first meeting with Travis. Arrangements were made with the bank, which was happy to refinance the mortgage. Eric and Helen resigned from their jobs. Within only a few short months the keys were in their hands and they were able to sit behind the counter of their *own* local bookstore and contemplate how lucky they had been.

Unfortunately, the time Eric and Helen's had to indulge in their 'dream' surroundings was all too short. Only three months after they had put their own names above the door, Eric had sought me out on a friend's recommendation. He needed help to work out what was going on. Something wasn't right: they weren't earning what they thought they would earn and they were going backwards quickly.

5 Clues That Your Relationship Is On The Rocks

It is always hard to break bad news to business owners like Eric and Helen. From the beginning they had made such an enormous emotional investment in their bookstore; hearing that their financial investment was in danger of collapse came as a genuine shock.

We spent some time together going over the financial statements they had been provided with during the sales process, and the real numbers that their business was producing now. First, on almost every line, they had either paid too much (or agreed to pay too much in the future), or the projections they had been provided with painted far too rosy a picture. Some of this was could be put down to overly optimistic numbers provided by Travis. In other areas Helen and Eric had just not had enough knowledge to understand what they were getting themselves into.

Second, there were some really basic flaws in the deal Eric and Helen had signed up to.

The rent that they were paying was too high compared with what similar sized businesses were paying in the same area. The franchise company had offered a standard rental arrangement in which the rental levels were those paid by stores in much busier locations. Eric and Helen hadn't bothered asking other businesses what they were paying, or checking in with local real estate agents: they had simply accepted what was on offer.

The purchase price for the business had included a sum for leasehold improvements: internal work done on the shop fit-out in the previous twelve months. That this should be paid for was reasonable – there was still plenty of depreciation claimable on these improvements. But the amount that was charged looked very high to me in comparison with what I have seen elsewhere. Again, Eric and Helen had not made any enquiries to ascertain the true value of what they were paying for.

They had also paid too much for existing Inventory. The stock figures they had received – the 'stocktake' – detailed the inventory-on-hand in some detail. What wasn't shown, however, was the *age* of the books in stock. It doesn't take a lot of imagination to understand that most books lose value over time. A five-year old novel, unless it is a 'classic', is unlikely to fetch its full original retail price, so its real value is somewhat less than its original value. And even classics are regularly spruced up by their publishers, making older stock look, well, old. Nearly a third of the stock in Eric and Helen's store fell into the 'aging' category, but they had paid full price for it. Potentially exacerbating the problem, Eric and Helen had accepted the Inventory valuation at face value. They had not made any attempt to check the accuracy of the stocktake figures.

Finally, the Inventory problem had been made worse since Eric and Helen had taken over the store. They had enthusiastically stocked up on new titles since they had taken over, creating similar Inventory problems to those Donna had, as we saw in Chapter 2. Bookshops are unusual when it comes to the way their Inventory is managed. Most books are provided by publishers or distributors on a 'sale or return' basis. This means that, while the stores pay for their Inventory, if it doesn't sell within a given period, the books can be returned for a full credit. This reduces the risk of being caught with old stock. It also encouraged Eric and Helen to stock up in the same way that Donna was enthused by wholesale discounts. But the extra books still had to be paid for, creating a drain on cash. Most of their older stock was well past the 'sale or return' deadline – it could no longer be returned for credit – further reducing its real value.

Few people would enter a marriage or any other long-term relationship without putting some level of diligence into getting to know their intended partner. Even Eric and Helen, who liked to tell me the story of how they knew they were right for each other from their first meeting, took some time to get to know each other well before they committed to marriage. Yet they were both willing to enter a serious financial commitment on the basis of what was, effectively, a first date. They had not done nearly enough of what the lawyers like to call 'due diligence': investigation into the real value and expected return of their intended purchase.

> **KEY POINT**
> **When buying or starting a business, every effort must be made to properly evaluate all aspects of the arrangement – to do thorough 'due diligence'. Never allow your emotions to cancel out the need for this investigation. Never take the figures provided by the vendor at face value.**

And where did these problems leave Eric and Helen? With higher Fixed Costs than the previous owner (due to the excessive rent), higher Liabilities (due to the bank loan taken out to pay for the business) and a lower average Gross Profit Margin (due to the fact that a large percentage of the Inventory could not be sold at the full retail price because it was old and not in demand by current customers). In the end, their Break-even was much higher, and their Gross Profit and Net Profit margins substantially lower, than they had being expecting. In terms of 'earning Ernest' and 'spending Penny', Eric and Helen's Penny was running much faster than they had expected and Ernest was running much slower. The net result was a wider initial gap between the two to begin with, and a lower 'catch up rate'. It was going to take a long time for Ernest to catch up to Penny under this scenario, if ever.

That wasn't the end of their problems, either.

It's Not You, It's ME

Because Eric and Helen had bought into the business before having their own superannuation money to invest in it, they had taken out a sizeable loan (via their mortgage) to finance the purchase of the business. Travis had been quick to tell them the advantages of borrowing money, but he hadn't been so open about the disadvantages.

As we discussed in the case of Bernie in Chapter 5, any investment in a business should always be made with the expectation of a financial return. In Bernie's case we were discussing the investment of cash (which becomes 'Equity' when it is injected into a business), as opposed to the investment of borrowings (which become 'Debt' or 'Liabilities') in Eric and Helen's case. Investing borrowings makes the need for a financial return both more important and more difficult at the same time.

Particularly when an investment is made with borrowings, it is more important that there is a positive financial return. If there isn't, the business will not be able to service the monthly repayments of principal and interest on the loan, and the loan will increase further in size. Eventually the size of the loan will outgrow the value of the underlying business, leaving – in Eric and Helen's case – the potential for loss of not only the business but also the Asset pledged to secure the loan with the bank (i.e., their home).

Even though Debt is a more leveraged way to grow a business (because you can borrow more than you have in cash to invest), it is more difficult to achieve a healthy financial return because, quite simply, *borrowing money costs money*. Unlike an Equity (i.e., cash) investment, Eric and Helen had to pay ongoing interest payments on their loan. This interest was an additional ongoing expense that (while known and able to be planned for) had not been properly factored into their initial calculations of Net Profit margin, Cash Flow and Break-even. Interest expense is a Fixed Cost which raises a company's Break-even point and additional Cash Flow will be required in order to make both principal and interest payments. Both need to be budgeted for.

Where the previous owner had been able to achieve a 10% return on their investment ('Return on Equity', or ROE, in the jargon of accountants), Eric and Helen would only make a 7.5% return on the same level of sales. Add to that the inflated price they had paid for the fit-out improvements and Inventory, and the actual 'Return on Equity' was lower still.

KEY POINT

When borrowing funds to buy or start a business, calculation of projected 'Return on Equity' (ROE), Net Profit Margin and Break-even must include all costs associated with that borrowing.

As with the inventory valuation and rental calculation, Eric and Helen had been given poor advice by Travis, but they had also been naive. They had been told that their Penny would run at a certain speed, but they hadn't taken the time and effort to work out what Penny's speed (given the size of the loan and the repayments to the bank) would equate to in their own circumstances – circumstances different to those of the previous owner who did not have a bank loan. It was like placing a bet on Penny to win a cross-country race, while only having ever watched her in a short sprint.

KEY POINT

Never assume that a business will perform in the same way for you as it did for the previous owner. Your financial circumstances will probably be different, and projections should be adjusted and re-calculated accordingly.

ꟹ

At some point – for the purpose of start-up, acquisition or expansion – every business owner must make a decision to either borrow funds or inject equity into a business. Equity can come from personal savings or from the cash of another third-party investor. Debt and equity both have dramatically different impacts on earnings, profitability, Cash Flow, Break-even, taxes, leverage and dilution (of the owner's control and interest in the company).

As a general guide, there are three key ratios, or KPIs, that business owners can use as a guide to manage and assess the balance of Debt to Equity in an enterprise and the effect on the overall profitability and Return on Investment. These are (1) Debt to Equity ratio (2) Return on Assets or 'ROA', and (3) Return on Equity or 'ROE'. Let's look at each one now with Eric and Helen's business in mind.

Debt To Equity = Total Liabilities / Total Owner's Equity

The Debt to Equity ratio simply indicates how many dollars of debt a company owes for every dollar of equity invested in the business.

The previous owner of Eric and Helen's bookstore did not have a loan with the bank so he had very low Debt or Liabilities. As a result, his Debt to Equity ratio was about 0.50, meaning he had only $0.50 of debt for every $1.00 of equity invested in the company. This is a low Debt to Equity ratio and meant that a bank would have assessed his business as low risk.

Eric and Helen, on the other hand, borrowed heavily from the bank in order to buy the business before they access to their superannuation money. The Debt to Equity ratio on the business after their purchase increased to 3: they had $3 of debt for every $1 of equity. Accountants call a business like this 'highly leveraged'. As a general rule of thumb, most banks will become concerned about your ability to service and repay a loan once your Debt to Equity ratio exceeds 2, that is, you have twice as much debt as you have equity.

ROA = Net Profit Margin x Asset Turnover

Return on Assets, or 'ROA', tells an investor how much profit a company generates for each $1 it has in Assets. In other words, it measures a company's earnings in relation to all of the resources it has at its disposal. ROA is the most stringent test of expected shareholder return and is used to gauge the 'Asset Intensity' of a business. Companies like car manufacturers, telecommunications providers and airlines are very 'asset intensive', meaning they require big, expensive machinery or equipment to generate a Profit. Such companies would typically have an ROA of 5% or less (that is, they generate only $0.05 for each $1 in assets). Conversely, graphic design firms, software companies and life or business coaching practices are generally 'asset-light'. Companies like these might have an ROA of 20% or more (that is, they generate $0.20 for each $1 in assets).

ROA is influenced by two equally important factors. The first is your Net Profit Margin (ie, the amount you make after covering all of your Fixed and Variable Costs) and the second is your 'Asset Turnover' (i.e., the ratio of Total Sales to Total Assets). Essentially, if you have $1 million in sales this year and Assets of $500,000, then your 'Asset Turnover' would be 2.0. The benchmark or target ROA will be different for companies in different industries because of 'Asset Intensity' differences like those I just described. But every company should endeavor to improve their ROA over time.

In the case of Eric and Helen, their ROA was much lower than expected (i.e., relative to the previous owner) for various reasons. Firstly, higher Fixed Costs (rent and debt repayments) and lower Gross Profit Margins (due to the percentage of old, unwanted stock) caused their Net Profit Margin to decrease. Secondly, they invested heavily in more, new stock which caused their overall Inventory (and total Assets) to grow at a much faster rate than Total Sales. This of course caused 'Asset Turnover' to drop accordingly. It is easy to see why overall ROA decreased: a smaller number (Net Profit Margin) multiplied by a smaller number ('Asset Turnover') will always result in a smaller answer (in this case, ROA).

ROE = Net Profit / Average Owner's Equity for Period

Return on Equity (ROE) is one of the most commonly used and important indicators of business profitability. It reveals how much profit a company earned in comparison to the total amount of Owner's Equity. Owner's Equity is equal to total Assets (what you own) minus total Liabilities (what you owe). It represents the net position of the owners in the business. Positive Owner's Equity is the business equivalent of having paid off your household mortgage; negative Owner's Equity is the equivalent of still having a mortgage to service.

Owner's Equity is (another) creation of accounting. It represents the value of assets created by the Retained Earnings of the business (i.e., the earnings not paid out, or the Profit reinvested in the business), plus the capital invested by the investors. In a business where there is no Debt or Liabilities, we would expect ROA and ROE to be the same amount.

Why is ROE so important? Simply put, a business that has a high ROE is more likely to be able to generate cash internally than a business with a low ROE. It is a measure of the business's ability to sustain itself, without the need for further injections of Equity or borrowings. For the most part, a high ROE is good. It is a good thing if a company's ROE is higher this year compared with last year, and/or if the ROE is higher the industry in general. In the case of Eric and Helen, both Net Profit and Average Owner's Equity decreased as a result of taking on the large bank loan. As Net Profit decreased, the overall ROE percentage went down and, with it, Eric and Helen's ability to generate enough cash internally to produce the same return as was enjoyed by the previous owner.

As a general rule of thumb, companies represented by the S&P 500, the biggest and best public companies in America, average ROE's of 10-15%. A business earning a Return on Equity in excess of 15% (especially in light of the recent economic downturn) would generally be thought to be outperforming the market.

Could a Threesome Help Your Business?

From a coach's or consultant's point of view it is always a bit tricky going into a business that has already been provided with external advice – especially when that advice was of dubious quality. In Eric and Helen's case, unfortunately, that's exactly what had happened. Travis might have appeared helpful but, perhaps because of his enthusiasm to sell the franchise, he had not been as helpful as he might have been. Eric and Helen, for their part, had been somewhat naive. They had accepted Travis's advice without question, and had not sought a second opinion from a qualified accountant or business coach at any stage. They had not, as I said earlier, done enough 'due diligence' before buying their business.

Eric and Helen were now in the position of having paid – with borrowed money – more than they should have for their franchised bookstore. The shop was not providing the level of return that they needed to sustain their standard of living.

Aside from explaining where they had gone wrong, there wasn't a lot of point in either of us dwelling on what might have been. I did point out that, should they expand this business or buy another one in the future, they would be wise to retain the services of a good accountant and a credible, experienced business coach to get clear picture of what the business looks like now and what it might look like in the future – in their unique circumstances. In fact, a good threesome – them, a qualified accountant and an online coaching tool like Businest® – would have minimized surprises and ensured they understood exactly what they were getting into. (Even though Businest® was originally designed to help owners enhance the profitability and Cash Flow of their existing businesses, it can be used by potential investors (and sellers) as an analytical tool to evaluate the financial position of a company based on at least two years worth of financial statements. Proper care must be taken to ensure that the veracity of the financial statements is established first. The Businest® reports will only be as good as the data used to compile them. If the underlying data is incorrect, incomplete or misstated, the reports will not reflect the true potential or return expected by the business.)

Why Failure to Communicate Can Hurt Your Venture Without You Even Knowing It

As for digging themselves out of the messy situation they had found themselves in, Eric and Helen had, broadly, three options.

The first option, and the one probably most in vogue in large corporates lately, was to drastically cut costs. Cutting Fixed Costs would, in theory, increase their Net Profit, which would, in turn, increase their Return on Equity and Return on Assets. They could, for instance, cut Fixed Costs by reducing staff, decreasing their administrative expenses or renegotiating the monthly lease payments. Or they could reduce their opening hours, thus reducing the power bills and other costs associated with running the business. But, as with most drastic cost cutting, there was a real risk of accidentally poisoning the business with the medicine used to treat the ailment. Reducing hours or staff might lead to lost customers and lower sales. And so on.

Substantial cost-cutting in a business is like cutting the lines of communication in a relationship that is already in trouble. The silence might calm things down for a while, but it is unlikely to have any long-term lasting benefit. It undermines the point of the relationship in the first place and, if sustained for any period of time, will only make things worse.

The second option, at the other extreme, was to try to expand the business quickly. Eric and Helen could try to rent another shop to expand their range, or just buy larger quantities of new, top-selling releases. They could introduce large discounts to try and increase sales. But in all these cases, as we saw with Serge in Chapter 1, increasing sales by these means would require spending (i.e., more Debt) which would only cause Penny to run faster. It would add to their overall Liabilities, increase their Debt to Equity and decrease their Return on Assets and Return on Equity. And in any case, increased Sales due to discounting would not have a positive impact on Gross Profit or Cash Flow.

Incurring more Debt in order to grow out of low Return on Equity or Return on Assets is like trying to fix a troubled relationship by sleeping around. It might make you feel better for a while, but it will do nothing for the original relationship and it will likely end in tears.

That left Eric and Helen with one option, which by this time they were ready to guess.

"When we have a disagreement," Helen said, "we have always worked to discuss it, to work it out by talking. Sometimes it takes a while, but better communication always works in the end. Is there a business equivalent?"

There is. It involves casting aside quick fixes like cost-cutting or attempting to grow too quickly through Debt, and instead working slowly but steadily on the underlying problems of the business. In Eric and Helen's case we targeted a number of specific things they could do straight away.

They held a sale to clear out a lot of their older inventory. It had been over-valued but there was little they could do about that now. The best they could do was to get rid of it. After the sale, which generated some welcome cash, they sold the rest of the old stock to a 'remainders' dealer who would on-sell it to those 'discount' bookstores you see around the place. The reduction in Inventory created Cash Flow, increased their Return on Assets (by increasing their 'Asset Turnover') and decreased their Debt to Equity (as they were able to pay down some of the debt with the money they made from the sale).

They negotiated some better payment terms with their suppliers for the following twelve months, giving them extra Cash Flow and some time to get their heads above the high water of their struggling business. They also managed to negotiate a temporary reduction in their rental payments which reduced their Fixed Costs and their Break-even point. The rent would still be owed, but would become payable when, hopefully, the business was more profitable.

And they took personal wage cuts which decreased their Fixed Costs and their Break-even point. This was not something they really wanted to do, but given their passion for the business, it was not hard to do either. In the end, Eric and Helen knew they would rather do it tough for a year or two than lose their dream business altogether.

And finally, instead of taking out advertising in the local paper, they started communicating every two weeks via email (for FREE) with their existing customers and they began to notice that repeat business increased and customers began to spend more money on average per transaction (i.e., upsales). Sales were starting to increase and Earnest was beginning to run faster while underlying advertising and marketing costs were decreasing, causing Penny to slow down in speed.

KEY POINT

If Return on Equity and Return on Assets are low, 'quick fixes' like cost-cutting or increased borrowing in isolation are unlikely to get things back on track. Patient, methodical improvement – focusing on strategies that will increase gross Profit Margin, stimulate repeat business, generate upsales and create Cash Flow – are what is needed.

With the financial shackles released just a little, Eric and Helen found themselves better able to relax into their store and to share their passion for books with their customers. They quickly built a reputation for fantastic service and their customer base began to grow as a result. It took time, but after about three years they found themselves earning what they had wanted to earn. When their superannuation finally became due, they were able to pay off their loans. When I last caught up with them, they were two of the happiest people you could meet.

Beware of the Rebound Relationship

Every business owner gets to this point eventually: the 'grass is always greener' point. Some let it pass. Some make a successful change. And some, like Rob, let it get them into trouble.

Rob had taken over his father's farm ten years before I met him. The mid-sized farm comprised mainly of mixed sheep farming, beef cattle and a few crops. It had been in Rob's family for three generations – three generations of conservative farmers who generally used good seasons to save for the inevitable bad ones.

The past few years had been good to Rob. Despite the ongoing drought, his farm had been blessed with enough rain to keep the business going without excessive spending on extra stock feed. He had made good decisions, with a bit of help from lady-luck, about when to fatten his animals, and as a result he had been able to achieve fair prices at the markets. And while the farm had never had a lot of debt, Rob had been able to pay off what remained and was now in the enviable position of owing the banks almost nothing.

Rob's problems started when he became a bit bored. Running the farm was becoming a bit routine. He denies that this was what prompted him to buy into the adjacent property when it came onto the market, but I have no doubt it was. His wife, Sarah, is sure it was.

"It's a great opportunity," Rob had told Sarah. "We may not have the chance again ... ever."

Sarah had agreed it was a rare opportunity, but she also felt that their current property was providing them with all the income they needed and that there wasn't really any need to expand. She had also pointed out that running the two farms, especially in a time of drought, would be a very large workload for Rob.

But Rob had sold himself on the idea and in the end Sarah had little choice but to support the decision. A visit to the bank – who were only too happy to support a long-standing customer like Rob – and he was ready to put up his hand at the auction. Two months later the property, and the new mortgage, were his.

ଓ

It was Sarah who asked me to come and see them. Her sister in the city had been at one of my workshops. I had not worked with a farming business before but I figured a business is a business: the basics are always the same. So I agreed to visit Rob and Sarah.

Their situation was really quite simple. Rob had borrowed money to buy the adjacent farm. At the time the title for the land was transferred, the new farm was not making any money. Rob had not bought any existing stock: all animals had been sold before the auction. Nor had he bought any crops: nothing had been planted for the current summer. All he had bought was a few thousand acres of farming land which had essentially been let go and was now in need of substantial work to make it productive again.

None of this was a problem for Rob from a farming point of view. There was no secret in what he was buying. He had only had to look over the fence at any time in the previous six months to see that nothing much was going on. Nevertheless, preparing land for pasture or crops was in Rob's blood. He could do it with his eyes closed.

But he couldn't do it without money – without cash.

By the time I met with Rob and Sarah, they had extended their friendship with the bank about as far as it would go. They had borrowed money on a long-term loan to buy the property. They had taken out another short-term loan, and an overdraft, to fund the first preparatory work on the new property: fuel for the tractors, seeds, fertilizer and the like, as well as wages for some extra casual labor to help out on the main farm while Rob worked on the new one. They had also almost reached all their credit card limits, and there was plenty more work to do.

Rob and Sarah were really in the worst-case scenario. In terms of their Ernest and Penny, they had a situation where Ernest wasn't moving at all – and wouldn't be for some months – but Penny was continuing to run away, almost out of sight. The gap between the two – the 'Cash Gap' – was growing wider at a fast rate. Without access to more cash very soon, they would default on their payments to the bank and potentially have to sell the new farm under 'fire sale' conditions.

KEY POINT
Having access to money or capital doesn't change the rules: Return on Equity always needs to be greater than the cost of capital or you risk going out of business backwards.

Rob had learnt a very harsh lesson. He had allowed boredom to draw his eyes to the adjacent property – but more to the idea of it than to the reality of it. He had allowed his emotions to dictate a buying decision; his emotions had driven him to ignore all the fundamentally conservative traits of his predecessors. And he had taken up an opportunity for what he saw as rapid growth – almost doubling his farm's size overnight – without thinking through the impact that growth was going to have on his Cash Flow. Increased growth doesn't just mean increased net profit. It also means that you will need increased Cash Flow upfront to support the growth and that cash must come from somewhere. In my coaching practice, I have seen more companies go out of business who were in high growth curves than in mature industries simply because they miscalculated and misunderstood the Cash Flow implications of expanding a business too quickly.

KEY POINT
Rapid growth is dangerous unless you are fully aware of the likely demands on Cash Flow and will be able to meet those demands.

In the end Rob had little choice but to re-mortgage his original farm. All his efforts to pay-off that mortgage over the previous ten years were undone with the flick of a pen. When I last spoke to him he had managed to get the new farm productive again and he was working his way forward, but it was going to be at least another decade – and quite possibly more unless the rains continued to be kind – before he got back to where he had been before his rash purchase.

Whip Your Business Into Shape NOW!

Yours or Mine? – Little Known Ways to Get the Debt vs Equity Balance Right In Your Business

- Calculate the Debt to Equity ratio in your business
  - Debt To Equity = Total liabilities/Total Owner's Equity
- Calculate the ROA ratio in your business
  - ROA = Net Profit Margin X Asset Turnover
  - Asset Turnover = Total sales/Average Assets for period
- Calculate the ROE ratio in your business
  - ROE = Net Profit / Average Owner's Equity for period
- What trends do you notice in these numbers over time (i.e., how do the numbers today compare to prior periods)?
- Set some realistic targets for what you would like these numbers to be within the next 90 days, 180 days and 365 days
- Find an accountant and a business coach who can help you to assess where you are at in terms of the Debt to Equity mix and assist you to get the balance right for your specific business
- Brainstorm at least three ways you can reduce Fixed Costs (increase your Net Profit Margin) in your business without negatively impacting sales
- Identify at least three ways to increase your Gross Profit Margin
- Generate at least three ideas to increase your Cash Flow
- Develop and implement at least three ways you can talk to existing customers (for FREE or very little cost) with the objective of getting them to shop with you more frequently
- Brainstorm at least three strategies to increase the amount of money customers spend with you when they are in your business (i.e., this is the equivalent of "do you want fries with that"?)
- Ask for a referral from each of your best customers – give them an incentive for bringing in new customers
- Send a thank you card to each of your best customers – studies have shown that a simple, hand-written thank you can increase business by between 10-18%

www.businest.com

CHAPTER 9

Under The Covers: Where The Fun Begins

Using S&M to whip your business into shape

(aka Learning to master statistics and measurement to drive business improvement)

In This Chapter

How Long Is A Piece Of String?

It Must Be Relevant

Make It Comparable

Benchmark It

Be Precise

Be Timely

Be Accurate

Make It Multi-faceted

Make It Available

"What information consumes is rather obvious: it consumes the attention of its recipients. Hence, a wealth of information creates a poverty of attention and a need to allocate that attention efficiently among the overabundance of information sources that might consume it."

Herbert Simon

Joseph, a recent client of mine, runs an animal hospital. Over a number of visits, I watched Joseph and his staff at work. I watched, in particular, the way they would methodically approach each new case.

There would be the initial questions of the owner: "What symptoms have you noticed?"; "When did you first notice this?"; "How much worse have things become?". These questions would be followed up by some sort of physical examination. Working gently, Joseph was a master of gaining feedback from an animal which couldn't speak back (obviously!) but could provide a response with the slightest flinch, the existence of a subtle swelling or a dull look in the eyes. Finally, if necessary, there would be the tests: blood tests, urine tests, x-rays and so on; sometimes more sophisticated tests had to be organized for a future date.

Drawing on a combination of all the information he had gathered, Joseph would make his diagnosis. From there he would prescribe some sort of remedy – ranging from drugs to the infamous 'bucket over the head'. In all but the simplest cases he would ask his client to return with the animal at some specified time in the future. On the follow-up visit, he would perform a streamlined version of the assessment he had made originally, comparing the results of the first examination with the more recent one. This would tell him whether or not any improvement had been made.

Joseph and his staff provided an excellent example of the importance of observation and measurement. The irony was that Joseph didn't understand the similar importance of measurement to his business.

On a number of occasions – doing something I do very often – I tried to get Joseph to go through his accounts with me. He would show me the standard reports sent by his accountant – the profit-and-loss, the Balance Sheet and so on. But he wasn't prepared to go 'deeper' with me – to spend time at the computer, delving into the 'numbers behind the numbers' of his business.

Finally I had to point out the unreasonableness of Joseph's approach. I placed an imaginary cat on his bench and asked him to examine the animal and tell me what was wrong with it ... but with restrictions. He could look at the cat, but he could not touch it. Nor could he turn it around or prompt it to move. Nor could he do any tests on it.

Joseph, always short of time, quickly became impatient with this game. "You're being ridiculous," he said. "This is totally unrealistic. How could any vet be expected to work under those conditions? It is only through examination and testing – going much deeper than what we can see on the surface – that we can make a thorough diagnosis."

"You are right. I agree absolutely." At this Joseph looked a bit taken aback, but I went on, "But do you realize that this is exactly what you are expecting me to do. You asked me to look at your business. You allowed me to have a look at it – even to watch you work. But you haven't found the time to give me any detailed financial numbers. You haven't allowed me to get 'under the skin', to prod and poke, to do any tests. And if you genuinely want some help with your business, we are going to have to do these things. Both you and I are going to have to operate on the numbers."

There are many analogies that can be, and very often are, used to underline the importance of measurement in tracking the progress of, and therefore running, a business. We can draw on sporting references, as I did in Chapter 7 when I used the tennis match to describe the importance of tracking Break-even. We can use aviation references: that 'flying' a business is like flying an aircraft – and no one would attempt to fly an aircraft without either clear visibility or a full suite of instruments. And we can use medical references, a variation on Joseph's story, describing how a doctor goes about performing a medical, diagnosing an illness or monitoring progress.

We can even use the analogy of Ernest and Penny: they have a very basic, visual measurement system to gauge the distance between each other, but without that basic system their race wouldn't be much fun.

Regardless of the analogy, the underlying point is very, very simple:

KEY POINT
If you want to succeed in business, you must effectively measure your progress.

But there is more to it than that. The great majority of smaller businesses, in particular, tell me something along the lines of: "But we do measure. Every month our accountant runs our financial statements. We get a Profit-and-Loss statement and a Balance Sheet. We even get an 'Aged Receivables' report so we can keep an eye on our Receivables." It may be the bookkeeper rather than the accountant, it may be quarterly rather than monthly, and the actual reports provided vary from time-to-time. The underlying theme, however, is that 'measurement' is something done once in a while, at some time after the fact, and in terms of the 'whole business', that is, not at any level of fine detail.

Measurement like this completely misses the point.

It is like playing a tennis match but only checking the score every hour – and even then looking at a score which is 20 minutes old. Or driving a car with your eyes closed and only looking, every few miles, at what your speed was a mile back. Or monitoring a heart attack victim by checking his charts two hours after the nurses have updated them.

Smart businesses take a very different approach. They use all the tools available to them and, if those aren't enough, find more tools that will tell them what they want to know, in a timely fashion, and in a format that is understandable and relevant. And it really isn't that hard to do.

How Long Is A Piece of String?
(aka The Who, What, When, Where and How of Good Measurement)

There are so many ways of measuring a business's progress that I could easily fill another book on this topic alone. The good news is that by focusing on the basics, and some fairly easy-to-calculate numbers and ratios, you will be a long way ahead of the Joseph's in this world.

Let's look some of the main characteristics of good measures in any business. To illustrate these points, we'll draw on examples from the case studies described in this book so far. These are not presented in any particular order; they are all important.

It must be relevant

You may have heard the saying *'What gets measured gets done'*. Equally important are the related statements *'You can only change what you measure'* and its sibling *'Don't measure what you can't act on'*. Collectively, these phrases are saying that you should choose measures which will drive your decision-making.

It was when Byron, the collectables retailer in Chapter 2 started to track the average age of his Inventory that he was able to reduce the number of older items which were tying up large amounts of cash. Similarly Frank, the furniture maker in Chapter 4, found that tracking his COGS and Gross Profit was as important as his partner Carlos's tracking of productivity measures on the factory floor. In both these cases, it was a failure to track these numbers that got my clients into trouble in the first place.

Make it comparable

An aspect of measurement which is often overlooked – even in larger businesses – is the importance of *ratios.*

A Gross Profit of $100,000 one month and $120,000 the next month looks good on the surface. But if those same figures were expressed as ratios of Gross Profit to Sales (ie, gross Profit Margin), say, you might find those same figures come out as 50% and 30% respectively. In other words, sales have gone up in the second month while COGS have increased considerably more to result in an overall decrease in Gross Margin profitability. These figures are not real, but if they were, they would flag potential problems with COGS like those which Carlos and Frank experienced.

Ratios can be used in most aspects of financial measurement to make numbers more comparable from one week or month to the next, regardless of variation in the 'busyness' of the business. 'Operating Expense Margin', the ratio of Operating Expenses to Sales, illustrates how the Fixed Costs of running your business are growing or falling as the sales rise and fall. Following 'Number of Days Inventory on Hand' – the ratio of the value of stock on hand to the average daily sales volume – would give Charlie or Carol in Chapter 2 an early indication of an unnecessary build up in Inventory, in a particular month. 'Turnover per Employee' allows you to track the impact of adding or removing staff. A figure I call 'Short Term Risk tells you how many dollars of cash or near cash you have to cover current liabilities as they come due' ... And these are just a few examples. Almost every measure you might care to track can be converted into one or more ratios to make it more useful.

Benchmark it

Ratios have the additional benefit of allowing comparison between one business and another, or between your business and 'average' figures for your industry. In other words, ratios can help you 'Benchmark'.

In Chapter 1, I described how Serge had put his spreadsheeting skills to good use in developing his price list. He had carefully included all his costs so that he knew each dish would be profitable. What I didn't talk about at that point was that I had also helped Serge Benchmark his prices. The typical café should expect to get an average of around 70% Gross Profit Margin (there's that ratio again). So, having calculated the raw cost of a dish at $3, Serge knew he had to charge about $10 (or 3.3 x the COGS) to arrive at a Gross Profit Margin of 70%. He adjusted some a little lower and some a little higher, but the overall average was about right. If a dish could not return a 70% Gross Profit (or thereabouts) while staying within his target price range of around $15 per main meal, it was either changed or deleted from the menu. There were not a lot of all-you-can-eat specials on Serge's menu as a result!

Because ratios 'cancel out' the size of a business from the equation, they are very useful benchmarking tools. They can help you objectively assess your performance to date and the trends over time of Gross Profit, Inventory levels, Receivables outstanding, Operating Expense Margins and so on. In this way, Businest® is particularly useful as a broad spectrum of KPIs are measured and benchmarked automatically for you and the anomalies and problem areas are highlighted for your immediate attention.

Benchmark numbers should only ever be taken as a guide: every business is unique in its own way and there will be variations. They can, however, play an important role in setting initial targets and in keeping you both competitive and profitable.

Be precise

One of the biggest drawbacks of relying on the standard Profit-and-Loss Statement and Balance Sheet as key measures of your business is their lack of precision. Sales, for instance, are typically presented as a total value without any breakdown into products, product groups or cash versus on account. This can cause confusion or, worse, misguided decision-making. In Todd's wholesale homewares business (Chapter 7), trouble arose when the mixture of sales drifted towards lower gross margin products. Todd and I eventually worked this out, but only by delving into the detail. The standard financial reports would never have illuminated this.

Precision can be applied in other ways too. Time, usually presented in a standard Profit-and-Loss Statement in 'chunks' of one month, can be much more usefully broken down into weekly or, preferably, daily bites. Todd did this with the implementation of his daily 'Break-even' and 'Break-even plus Profit' targets. By measuring these with the precision of a day, instead of a month, Todd was better placed to react to any sudden threat or opportunity.

Another example of precision being put to good use was in Craig and Mandy's plumbing business (in Chapter 3). Mandy demanded that her plumbers record material and time usage by the specific job. This made her invoicing easier, but it also helped her reduce her Receivables problem by separating out any part of a job that was missing a purchase order. She wouldn't have been able to do this without enormous effort had she had not collected precise information from her team members.

Precision can also be used in the way you look at your numbers, by looking at smaller and smaller 'slices'. For example, one of the measures I encourage many clients to develop is 'Profit per hour per employee'. This is often calculated backwards by breaking down the aggregated daily profit figure by the total number of employees and the total number of hours worked in the period. It gives a very precise measurement of how much profit is actually earned by the business each and every hour it is open and it is an excellent KPI for an owner to track if he or she is absent from the business for a period of time.

Be timely

It is often said that running a business off the financial statements is like driving a car while looking in the rear view mirror. Even with computing power being what it is today, the 'month end' period for most businesses – the time when accounts for the month are finalized – remains at least a few days, if not a couple of weeks after the period is over. It is impossible to use data effectively under these circumstances. If a problem arises at the start of a month, you may not pick it up until *six weeks* later, by which time it is far too late to react. And if you do react, you won't know whether your change was beneficial or not for another few weeks. This was the sort of situation that caused angst for Todd, for Frank and Carlos, for Pamela in her mobile catering business and for Eric and Helen in their bookstore. It wasn't until I worked with each of these clients and developed measures they could review on a regular basis – built from fresh data – that they started to get full control of their businesses.

The best example we had of 'untimely' data management was Jason the electrician. In Chapter 1 we saw how keeping his paperwork inside his van and not processing his invoices for several weeks, he was stretching out the time it took to get paid. But he was also creating a situation in which there was no way he could gain an accurate picture of his business's health. His standard financial statements would not have shown a true picture because they wouldn't have included sales made but not invoiced. And even if he had had better 'ratio-based' measures set up, they would have painted a false picture too – again because they were missing data.

Timeliness is one reason why most businesses use the 'accrual' accounting method we discussed in the box 'Profit versus Cash Flow' in Chapter 1. By recording (accruing) sales made but not collected, and purchases made but not yet paid for, a company is able to work off more timely numbers.

Aside from accrual, the best thing you can do to ensure you are processing and recording all transactions (both sales and purchases) as quickly as possible in an accounting software program like MYOB or Quickbooks.

Be accurate

It should hardly need to be said that any measurements you are using to make decisions about your business should be based on accurate data. The truism often used about accuracy is *'Rubbish in ... rubbish out'*, which means that the value you get from your data is directly related to its accuracy. Yet time and time again I find myself in businesses where accuracy is a second-class citizen.

The most common sources of inaccurate data are where human intervention is involved. And of these the most troublesome of all is Inventory.

While larger businesses account for Inventory by recording each change as it happens (as the supermarkets do, for instance, when they scan goods at the checkout), smaller businesses often rely on irregular stocktakes – inventory counts – to keep their records straight. The problem is that counting of inventory is time-consuming, so it is often put off, and even when it is done there is ample scope for error unless the counters really know what they are doing. Imagine, for instance, counting the stock in Carol's beauty salon (Chapter 2). All those shampoo bottles which look the same but for a subtle color variation and some fine print at the base. It would take an experienced person to count those bottles accurately.

But accurate inventory records are essential, especially if Inventory is a large component of your business. Sudden, unexpected changes in Inventory can flag a problem with shrinkage, for example, as in Pamela's food van business (also Chapter 2). And tracking a figure like the 'number of days of inventory on hand' – a very useful measurement – is pointless unless your Inventory data is accurate.

Accuracy is also important when making calculations. In Carlos and Frank's furniture business, unnoticed changes in the raw material price caused them to be making pricing decisions based on inaccurate data. It wasn't until those price increases had been identified that corrections could be made.

Make it multi-faceted

Throughout this book our case studies have focused on specific areas of concern: Inventory, Receivables, Return on Equity etc. In practice, of course, everything is tangled up together. Inventory affects Cash Flow, as do Receivables. Receivables are affected by Terms, which can affect Pricing. Pricing affects Break-even and Return-on-Assets, as do Costs of Goods Sold (COGS). And so on.

Just as driving a car requires that you combine observation with a feel for the car and feedback from the instruments, so it is that a combination of measures is needed to drive a business. To revisit our tennis analogy, the same applies there. The scoreboard is one measure, but a good player will be monitoring her fitness, identifying her most common sources of errors and analyzing her competitors' weaknesses too.

So does this mean that you need to keep your eye on everything? Well, no ... and yes.

The smarter business operators I've worked with become good at focusing on different measures at different times, while keeping a watchful eye over other general areas. So Serge, in Chapter 1, started to focus on Cash Flow over sales, while obviously not ignoring the latter altogether. Byron, in Chapter 2, focused on the age of his Inventory while, again, keeping an eye on overall Inventory levels, Cash Flow and so on.

The trick is to focus on areas of particular, current vulnerability – a point I'll come back to. At the same time, though, effective business management means being able to keep your eyes on a few dials at a time, and understand the relationship between those readings.

Make it available

The final characteristic of good measures is, strangely, the least relevant to the data but the most important to success.

In addition to meeting all the criteria I've discussed above, any measurement you make must be readily available to you. That means that you need to be able to access it quickly and easily and in a format that is understandable and useful.

There are two reasons for this. First, if you can't measure something easily, you will eventually stop measuring it at all. (Don't pretend otherwise – it always happens that way.) Second, if it can't be measured easily, you'll find yourself spending too much time measuring and analyzing and not enough time running your business.

Another aspect of availability is that you need to be able to do the measurement yourself. If, like many businesses, you rely on sending your data to an accountant or bookkeeper, who keeps it for a week before sending it back, then you will never have real control of your business. It's like expecting a relationship to endure constant, lengthy physical separations – it can work, but only with a lot of luck.

To summarize then, 'available' data is easy to capture often, easy to analyze, and easy to process by yourself (or at least by an in-house staff member). And it will meet all the requirements above.

Is this an easy point to get to? Not really – or at least not until now. It is because this has always been so hard to achieve that it is so seldom done. This is why so many business owners are flying through clouds with their eyes closed and hoping for the best.

A final point on measurement. Measurement, while critically important, is never a replacement for *action*. But it can play an important role in encouraging action to happen and ensuring it is focused on the right tasks.

In my first book, *On the Shoulders of Giants*, I talked about the concept of the Reticular Activating System (RAS). The RAS is part of the brain, and one of its main roles is as a 'filtration system'. Its role is to shield our consciousness from all the 'noise' around us. It helps keep at bay all the sounds, images, ideas and information which swirl around our lives but which aren't immediately relevant to us. In the book I described how the RAS means that we tend not to notice pregnant women until the day we learn we are expecting a baby ourselves. At that point, the RAS pulls pregnant women to the front of your awareness and suddenly you notice them everywhere.

In business, focused measurement can play the same role as getting pregnant – so to speak. Focusing measurement on a particular area of vulnerability or concern can raise the profile of that area and encourage action. So Serge's focus on Cash Flow caused him to see everything in that light. If he added a new product, he considered its affect on Cash Flow. If he had to hire an emergency staff member from an agency, he focused his attention on the Cash Flow implications of paying the agency. Cash Flow, for Serge, was everywhere.

A similar thing happened to Pamela (Chapter 2) when her shrinkage problem became apparent. Product theft had not been on her radar at all – her RAS had filed the idea of shrinkage as unimportant – which is why she didn't see it coming. Once it appeared on her radar, she took action to stamp out shrinkage. She removed the staff member concerned, and she put into place more careful measurement of inventory levels so that stealing would be discouraged in future instance and, if it did happen, it would be revealed more quickly.

There are a million actions you could take to improve your business, but there will never be time to do them all. Using measurement to spark your Reticular Activating System into action can help you choose which of all those possible actions you will take. When this sort of filtering takes place, all the jobs you have to do can seem much less overwhelming because you can focus your time and resources on the items that will give you the best return on your effort.

Just one more thing, while we're here. Once a problem is 'solved', you shouldn't remove your focus entirely. When Eric and Helen finally got their Inventory under control again, I didn't tell them they could forget about Inventory now. Just because a problem is fixed for now doesn't mean it is fixed for good. Inventory remained an important thing to watch carefully for Eric and Helen even as they turned more attention towards increasing their Gross Profit margin. Your RAS can help here too: once it brings something into your field of view, it won't let go too quickly.

Using a systemized measurement and information system like Businest® will enable you to pinpoint pain in your organization and thus simplify and direct your attention to focus on what will return the biggest improvement. MYOB (or any accounting system) is all about 'measurement' whereas Businest® is about 'improvement'. We take the hassles and overwhelm out of tracking your KPIs and trying to figure out what is most important and pressing. Businest® is simple, easy-to-understand, fun, powerful and interactive. It's like giving your business a good kick up the RAS!

www.businest.com

CHAPTER 10

It's Not "Them", It's You!

Why you're the biggest obstacle in your business

In This Chapter

Lack of Accountability

Lack of Focus

Fear of Financials

Failure to Measure

Perfectionism

Refusing To Let Go Of The Past

Constantly Comparing Yourself to Others

""What lies behind us and what lies before us are tiny matters compared to what lies within us."

Oliver Wendell Holmes

You have met a wide range of my clients in this book, most of whom I can report made real differences to their businesses by taking focused, targeted action in the problem areas we were able to identify. There have been others, I will admit, who didn't make the book because their stories weren't as positive.

It wasn't that these less successful clients were in worse situations than the ones described in this book. In fact some of them were much better off than, say, Eric and Helen, or Charlie – clients who were genuinely teetering on the edge of the cliff when I met them.

The difference is that some clients take their challenges in their stride and work to deal with them. The others fall into what I call self-sabotage: subconsciously holding themselves back by allowing the world to dictate terms and then blaming everyone and everything else when nothing goes right.

You can tell a lot about a business person and their tendency for self-sabotage by the way they spend their time. We all spend our time in various ways. Many business owners tell me that there is not enough time in the day to get everything done. I, on the other hand, have a belief that there is always enough time in the day to do all of the things that are WORTH doing. The key is to identify what is worth your while. Sometimes activity can be a kind of anesthesia for the pain of not achieving the results you want and deserve. Action is always better than procrastination. However, more activity is not always better than less.

Everyone knows that 90% of what you and I do every single day is purely habit, good or bad. Have you ever noticed just how many of your everyday activities are just deeply ingrained habits? Driving your car, putting on your watch, brushing your teeth or taking a shower. You wouldn't dream of not doing these things – they are part of your routine and they just seem to happen automatically. In your business you will have similar habits such as checking your email, opening the mail, grabbing a coffee or talking about the weekend's sporting upset. You do these things without conscious thought – they just happen.

Then there is the time spent on 'make busy' activities. If you've ever spent your day stuck in back-to-back meetings, answering routine questions from your team, responding to emails, troubleshooting, emptying the in-tray or tidying the office, you know exactly what I mean by 'make busy' activities.

It is easy to spend large amounts of time on habitual and 'make busy' activities. In fact it is possible to spend *all* your time on these activities, creating the magnificent illusion that you are hard at work, simply because you feel 'flat out'. Your day is full of tasks and you get home exhausted – so you must have been busy, right?

Unfortunately, these habitual and 'make busy' activities can keep you trapped where you already are – just simply maintaining, not growing your business. By filling your days with these tasks, you are in effect avoiding the very activities that you know will really move your business forward and produce tangible results – what we might call 'productive activities'.

Productive activities include the types of actions I have described my clients as taking in this book. Things like getting the invoicing done, doing a stocktake, setting up a simple inventory management system, following up on outstanding debts, reviewing your pricing structure or implementing some effective measurements. These are all actions which rarely happen 'automatically'. They require focused attention. And, all too often, they get relegated to 'tomorrow' or 'sometime soon'.

A great many business owners, while they like to think of themselves as entrepreneurial, would rather do anything other than face the thought of 'productive activities'. They probably have these things on their 'to do' lists, but after another day of busyness, they just say to themselves – again – "It's OK, I was really busy. The review of Fixed Costs will have to wait for tomorrow."

The problem is this – and believe me, I have seen it played out many, many times: if you are waiting for the right or best time to do these critical 'productive activities', that time will simply never come. Tomorrow there will be more 'busy work' to do, and your unproductive habits will fill the rest of the day, and the cycle will start all over again.

The business owners I have met who have been prone to self-sabotage are all stuck in this cycle. They allow their time to be soaked up by habits or by the demands of others. Then they find external causes to blame for their inability to change and their ultimate lack of success.

By contrast, the sorts of people you have met in this book – people who encounter challenges but overcome them – these people make time to focus on 'productive activities'. They rise above the 'noise' of busyness, create ways to focus their Reticular Activating System on the things that really matter *right now*, and get on with the job. They set specific goals and they monitor and take action based on the financial trends in their business. They don't try to do 'everything', they focus on the very things that will give them the most leveraged and positive result. They ultimately make doing these important activities an ingrained habit of a much more powerful kind. They rarely blame external circumstances when things go wrong, seeing them, rather, as out of their control and therefore not worth expending too much energy on.

☙

Let's look at some of the more common self-sabotage habits which could be holding you back right now in your own business.

Lack of accountability

It is one of the great freedoms of being a small business owner: the fact that you are your own boss. Being 'your own boss' is probably the main reason you went into business for yourself in the first place. But there is a downside. Having no one to account to often leaves business owners susceptible to self-sabotage. They revert to their teenage selves: "If no one is watching, I can muck around as much as I like". Sure, your family might complain if you don't make any money, but you'll probably give them the same excuses you are giving yourself. And they won't be in a position to challenge you.

It is always better to have someone else, whether it be a business partner, external advisor or coach, who can really pin you down on the difficult questions and tasks.

Lack of focus

I meet a lot of people in business who just allow things to roll along at their own pace, who are quite happy to take things as they come and see where their business grows. Then, when they get into trouble, they blame the circumstances that caused the trouble. To some extent they are right – by operating with a 'hands-off' approach, they certainly can't point the finger at their own actions. But they misunderstand business and the power of their own mind. They fail to see that having clear goals, and taking focused action to achieve those goals, largely isolates a business from the perils of external factors. Outside factors are not as important to the health and success of your business as what is going on right now in your own mind.

The best example of this we have discussed was Eric and Helen with their bookstore (Chapter 8). They could easily have given up their business by the time I saw them, blaming the bad advice they had received initially and tough economic times. But their strong belief, the passion for the lifestyle they were looking for, their willingness to listen and their courage to confront the brutal truth of their financial circumstances, gave them the determination and focus needed to, slowly, remedy their situation.

Fear of financials

Financial success underpins everything you want to achieve in your business – even if making a lot of money isn't your primary goal. If you are not covering the basic costs of operating your business and taking home a reasonable wage, you have effectively bought yourself a job – you are not a real business owner. Hopefully having now read this book you can see why that is. Unfortunately comfort with the financials is rare amongst small business owners. Most people – including everyone you've met in this book – went into business because they had a passion for what the business did, or, as in the case of Anthony in the printing business (Chapter 5), they were literally born into the business. Financial acumen is rarely seen as a prerequisite for business ownership. Instead it is seen as something to be ignored or outsourced. "I get my accountant to worry about that" is a phrase often heard. It's not enough.

Handing control of this major element of your business success to someone else is, again, a recipe for self-sabotage. When something goes wrong, it is too easy to say, "but my accountant didn't tell me". Finance is not something to be frightened of. As we've demonstrated in this book, a basic understanding requires only simple math skills. Finance is no more scary or difficult than learning the rules and scorekeeping for any other game or sport you might choose to play or indulge in – poker, football, motorsport, Nintendo, Pictionary, ballroom dancing etc.

Failure to measure

Often as a result of the just-mentioned 'fear of financials', but also because 'productive activity' is required to make this happen, a lot of businesses operate without meaningful measurement. I covered this topic pretty thoroughly in Chapter 9 so won't reiterate it all here. Suffice to say that a failure to monitor the progress of your business, and then to blame circumstances when you're hit between the eyes with a nasty surprise loss, is self-sabotage at its finest.

Remember Todd, in Chapter 7? Todd didn't like finding out, after the event, that he was failing to Break-even. He could have got lost in busyness and done nothing, after which the same thing would probably have happened the next month. But he didn't. He took action and put into place a much better measurement system. He took control by doing this, and removed the source of the nasty surprises.

Perfectionism

This is an insidious source of self-sabotage. It comes in two forms. The first is the tendency to do nothing until the circumstances are *just* right. As the circumstances are rarely 100% ideal, this form of perfectionism effectively immobilizes a business, hampering the ability to make decisions, start new projects or make any meaningful change. The second form of perfectionism is very common among small business people. It is the sense that no-one else can do the job to your exacting standard, so you must do it ALL yourself. As there will never be enough time to do everything, jobs get left undone.

Self-sabotage of this type reveals itself in the complaint that "you can't get good help these days". With attitudes like this, Serge's café would have closed within weeks of opening. His more experimental attitude – even if it was misguided at times – gave him the flexibility to work his way out of trouble. Pamela, with her food van business (Chapter 2), would never have got anywhere without the trust she showed in her staff. Sure, that trust was misguided in one instance, but she didn't allow herself to be hamstrung by one bad experience. She simply took action that allowed her to 'plug the hole' without completely locking down the business.

Refusing to let go of the past

Have you ever heard yourself say "we've always done it this way"? Or have you ever simply avoided doing something that you know you should have done because "last time I tried that, it didn't work"? Holding on to the past like this is another illustration of self-sabotage. The past does not necessarily equal the future – but it will, if you refuse to let go of it and continue to do what you have always done. Circumstances change and the only way to test an apparently good idea in today's conditions is to try it out. Frank learnt this in his furniture business. While his partner, Carlos, was busy making improvements in the factory, Frank had assumed that the pricing formulas of the past would continue to work. But when circumstances changed, so did the validity of his pricing structure. Rather than stubbornly refusing to change, he restructured his pricing and got the business back on track.

Constantly comparing yourself to others

While there is obviously some benefit to being aware of what's happening in your industry, and the tactics of your competitors, taking this comparison too far is another source of self-sabotage. Just as circumstances change with time, they are also unique for every player in your market. Some have been in the game longer, some shorter. Some have had a bit of luck and won a big contract, or developed a product that just happened to catch on.

It's important to look at the whole picture – good and bad. When Anthony and his sales team were tempted to add a digital printing machine to their offering "because that is what everyone else is doing", they failed to consider the big picture. They looked at the business that other digital printers were earning, but they didn't look at how much competition those printers were battling or how small their margins were. When they understood this, the digital market didn't look so attractive in comparison with their existing market.

ᘓ

If, as you've read this book, you've found yourself saying "that wouldn't work for us" or "our circumstances are different" or "this is too complicated – I'll leave it to my accountant", then I suggest you re-read the section above and isolate the sources of self-sabotage that you might be suffering from – your own unproductive habits. And then take action.

Unfortunately, there are few quick fixes in business. If you are prone to any of the above self-sabotage habits, it will take some concerted effort on your part to overcome them. These common forms of self-sabotage are deeply ingrained behaviors that take time to establish – and to eliminate.

In the 1960s a highly regarded plastic surgeon, Dr Maxwell Maltz discovered that it took 21 days for amputees to cease feeling phantom sensations in their amputated limb. From further observations and significant research he established that it takes 21 days to create a new habit. Brain circuits take engrams (which are essentially 'memory traces') and produce neuroconnections and neuropathways only if they are bombarded for 21 days in a row. This means that our brain does not accept new data or information for a change of habit unless it is repeated each day (without fail) for at least 21 days.

Changing habits (whether positive or negative) can be done but it takes time and consistent effort for at least 21 days. This can be hard to do on your own, which is why I highly recommend finding an objective person – preferably someone outside of your business – to hold you accountable to your plan, actions and results.

Ultimately, business is really quite simple. Regardless of what your product or service is, or what industry you are in, everyone makes money in the same way – we sell things to customers for money, which we collect and use to pay for Fixed Assets, Fixed Costs and Variable Expenses. The nuances and details might be different but the financial calculations and ratios are computed in the same way for ALL businesses. Net Profit is Net Profit, Cash Flow is Cash Flow. In a way, keeping score in business is a lot more straightforward than some sports – there are no dodgy calls by umpires nor marks for 'artistic impression'. Numbers don't lie – either you are making money or you are not. And if you are truly serious about being successful in business, and it is not just a hobby or a way to pass the time, you will find a way to fit a bit of Financial Foreplay® into your day so that you can whip your business into shape and start taking home more cash today!

Where to start? Put a sign on your door today – **"DO NOT DISTURB – FINANCIAL FOREPLAY® IN PROGRESS"** – and get to work!

APPENDIX I

About the Author

Rhondalynn Korolak has a creative and inspiring story that proves that you can **SEE, DO** and **HAVE** anything you set your mind to. From humble beginnings and despite formidable obstacles, to success as a leader and entrepreneur, Rhondalynn is one of the most dynamic and inspiring speakers on business acceleration, profitability and leadership.

A 16-year veteran of sales, marketing and finance, Rhondalynn holds degrees and professional designations in law and chartered accounting and she is a certified Master Practitioner of NLP, Thought Field Therapist, Clinical Hypnotherapist and Psychotherapist. Her CV features an impressive list of accomplishments in senior executive positions with Macleod Dixon, Price Waterhouse Coopers, Max Factor, Covergirl, Village Cinemas Australia, FlyBuys and Coles Group Ltd.

Her methodologies are engaging and memorable – she has an uncanny ability to inspire owners and managers to look at their businesses and financials in a completely new, practical and powerful way. Rhondalynn has a natural talent to motivate, lead and empower others to unlock and achieve their full potential – both personally and professionally.

She has been featured in national business publications, on prime time TV and radio stations across North America and Australia. She writes for numerous websites, blogs, magazines and eZines.

Rhondalynn speaks annually to thousands of entrepreneurs, sales professionals, senior executives, franchisees, sporting clubs, corporate employees and industry association members on the principles of leadership, business acceleration and mental toughness.

As an entrepreneur, Rhondalynn founded Imagineering Pty Ltd and Businest Pty Ltd to serve the growing demand for customized training,and coaching solutions based on leading edge, scientifically proven technologies. That mission is realized via seminars, training events, proprietary online financial software and coaching curriculums that ignite the quest for self mastery while offering practical and proven techniques to rise above challenges and realize your deepest dreams and potential.

Get To Know Rhondalynn

Follow Rhondalynn on Twitter - http://twitter.com/imagineeringnow

Visit Rhondalynn's Blog at http://imagineeringnow.com/category/blog/

Become a fan of Rhondalynn Korolak and "Financial Foreplay" on Facebook http://www.facebook.com/RhondalynnKorolak

APPENDIX II

Visit Our Website

busineSt
The safest place to grow your business

What does it cost you each month **NOT** to have answers to these important questions?

When do I cover all my costs each month and start making profit?

What is the impact on cash flow if I increase or decrease sales by 10%?

Can I afford to give a discount of 10% to close this sale?

Where should I spend my time and energy as an owner?

What is the BEST and quickest way to improve my results?

How much revenue does each team member contribute and can I afford to hire another?

Sign up for Businest®
www.businest.com

businest

The safest place to grow your business

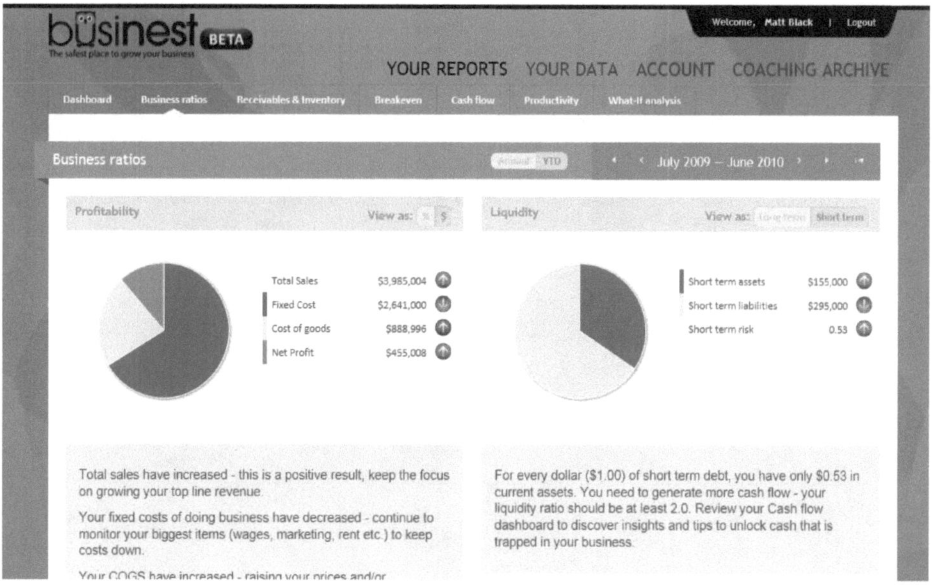

Want to quickly assess the financial health of your business so that you can work **ON** your business (and not just IN it)?

Sign up for Business®
www.businest.com

businest

The safest place to grow your business

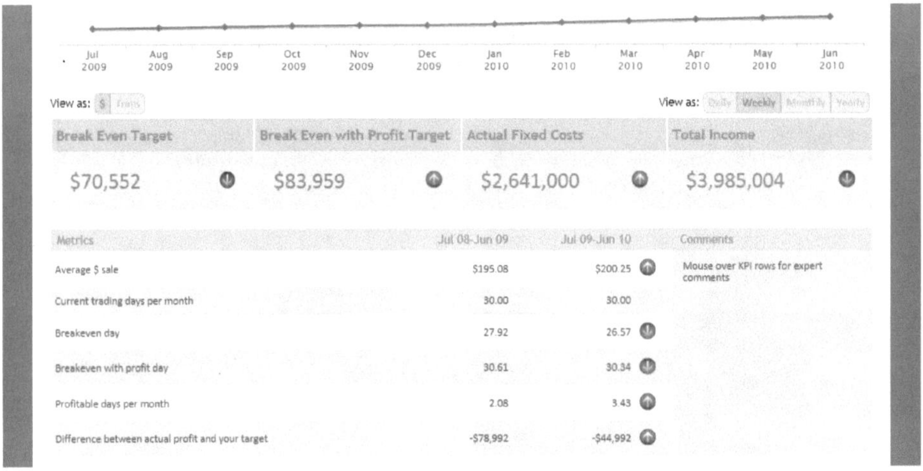

Which day of the month do you break even?

How many days of the month are you putting money in your own back pocket?

Discover what you and your team can do to increase the number of days you earn profit each month.

Sign up for Business®
www.businest.com

Business® goes beyond the reports from your accounting package, to analyse your financials and provide valuable insights which will enable you to make informed decisions, become a better leader and achieve the financial results you deserve.

Visit www.businest.com to whip your business into shape and take home more cash.

Sign up for Business®
www.businest.com

APPENDIX III

Glossary

Glossary of Financial Terms

Accounts Payable
The amount of money that a company owes to its suppliers at a given moment. Also known as 'Payables'.

Accounts Receivable
The amount of debt that is owed (outstanding) to a company by its customers at a given moment. Also known as 'Receivables'.

Accrual
An entry or adjustment in a company's accounts recording a sale or purchase made but not yet settled (i.e. cash receipt or payment that has not yet been made).

Accrual Accounting
A method of accounting in which revenues and expenses are recorded at the time they are incurred, regardless of when the corresponding cash is actually exchanged.

Aged Payables
Aged payables are those for which the due date for payment has already passed. An aged payables report will typically group the total amounts owed to suppliers into periods of 0 to 30 days (outstanding), 30 to 60 days, 60 to 90 days, and beyond 90 days.

Aged Receivables
Aged receivables are those for which the due date for collection has already passed. An aged receivables report will typically group the total amounts owed by customers into periods of 0 to 30 days (outstanding), 30 to 60 days, 60 to 90 days, and beyond 90 days.

Asset
Something of value owned or owed to a company.

Asset Turnover
The ratio of Total Sales divided by Total Assets.

Audit
An independent examination of an organization's financial records and accounts.

Authorized Share Capital
The highest amount of share capital that a company has been authorized to issue by the shareholders, as set out by the company's memorandum of association.

Bad Debt
Money owed by a customer that is not collectable (i.e. will never be paid).

Balance
The amount of money held in, or owed to, a bank account at any point in time. The balance is shown at the end of any bank statement.

Balance Sheet
A summary of a company's assets (what a company owns) and liabilities (debts a company owes) at a point in time (the Balance Sheet date).

Bankrupt
A situation where an individual or company does not have enough money to pay debts owing, declared by a court order.

Break-even
The point at which the cost or expenses of operating a business and the revenue from sales are equal: there is no net loss or profit.

Benchmarking
Method of assessing a company's performance by comparing it against historical trends, competitors or other industry ratios.

Budget
A summary of estimated revenue and expenditures over a certain period of time. Often includes a proposal for financing the expenditures.

Borrow
To obtain money on loan with the promise or understanding of returning it (or something equivalent) in the future.

Capital
The share of a company's assets that are owned by shareholders after all liabilities have been accounted for.

Capital Expenditure
Money a business spends on buying or improving its fixed assets, such as equipment or furniture (as opposed to money spent on the day-to-day operating expenses of the business).

Capital Gain
Money a business or person gains when a long-term asset, such as a building, is sold for more than it cost.

Cash Flow
The movement of cash through a business as it operates, including cash received as payments or capital (cash inflows), and cash paid out as operating or capital expenses (cash outflows). 'Positive' Cash flow for a period means more cash inflows than cash outflows over that period.

Cash Flow Statement
A statement summarizing a business's cash inflows and cash outflows - and the difference between them - over a period of time.

Cash Gap
A cash gap occurs when you pay out money to suppliers for goods/services before you have collected the money from your customers.

Cash Inflow
An amount of cash coming into a business, usually as payment (by customers) for goods or services provided, or as a capital payment.

Cash Outflow
An amount of cash leaving a business, usually as payment (by the business) for goods or services received.

Check
A written order, addressed to a bank, instructing the bank to pay an amount of money to the person or organization named on the check.

Collateral
An asset offered to a lender as security for a loan. In the event that the borrower defaults on the loan, the lender will take ownership of the collateral. (A common example of collateral is the title to a home on which the bank has extended a mortgage.)

Contract
An agreement between two or more parties, which is usually written and is binding on everyone concerned.

Cost of Goods Sold (COGS)
All materials costs and expenses which can be directly attributed to the production of the goods produced or sold. Usually includes the cost of materials and direct labor.

Credit
Time given to a customer to pay for the goods or services supplied.

Credit card
A card that lets a person buy something 'on credit' and pay for it later.

Credit Reference Agency
An organisation holding information on a person and their past record of paying back their debts.

Credit Card Bill
A detailed statement each month of what a person has bought with their credit card and how much they need to pay back.

Credit Risk
The risk that a person or business might not repay a loan or pay an outstanding bill.

Credit History
A history of how well a person or business has been able to repay debt.

Credit Limit
The highest amount a store card or credit card company will lend a person or business at a given moment.

Credit Outstanding
The amount of credit a person has not yet paid back.

Credit Rating
A score of a person's or business's ability to repay debt such as loans and credit card bills (i.e. a score of credit risk).

Creditor
A person or company who is owed money.

Current Asset
An asset expected to be turned into cash within one year of the Balance Sheet date.

Current Liabilities
Short-term debts that a business must pay within a year, such as bank overdrafts, money owed to suppliers (Accounts Payable), goods and services tax and employees' income tax.

Current Ratio
Current Assets divided by Current Liabilities.

Debit
A payment or transfer from an account.

Debt
Money owed by a person or company to another person or company This could include money owed for goods and services (Receivables) or any funding which has a specified term and rate of interest.

Debtor
A person or company who owes money.

Debt to Equity Ratio
Total debt divided by total equity.

Depreciation
The amount by which the value of a tangible asset is deemed to have fallen (due to wear and tear, age, going out of date, etc.) during a particular period. Depreciation is an accounting adjustment and a non-cash expense.

Dividend
Money that a company pays to its shareholders out of the retained profit of the company.

Discount
Money that is taken off the price of something.

Equity
The difference between the value of the assets of a company and the total liabilities owed by the company Also used in reference to funding that is raised by a company in exchange for shares.

Expenditure (or Expense)
Any cost incurred which reduces the profits of a particular period.

Financial Statement
A statement that includes the annual financial numbers, directors' report, auditor's report etc. of a company.

Financial Year
The year covered by a set of financial statements.

Fixed Asset
An asset that a business intends to use for several years, like buildings and equipment.

Fixed Cost
An expense which does not change with small changes in the volume of goods sold or produced Fixed costs generally include rent, wages for full time employees, rates, taxes, insurance etc.

Gross Profit
Total sales less Cost of Goods Sold.

Gross Profit Margin aka 'Gross Margin' or 'Profit Margin')
Gross Profit as a percentage of sales.

Income Tax
A tax on personal or business income.

Income
Money coming in to a business (i.e. sales revenue or turnover).

Income Statement or 'Profit and Loss Statement')
A statement detailing a business's income and expenses for a period. In accounting terms, this statement shows how the profit attributable to shareholders in a given period was achieved..

Intangible Assets
Assets that cannot be 'touched', such as goodwill and patent rights.

Interest
A fee a person receives if they save money, or pay if they borrow money, usually expressed as a percentage of the total savings/loan.

Interest Rate
The percentage that a person or business receives on their savings or pays on a loan.

Issued Share Capital
The amount of the authorized share capital that has actually been issued/ given to its shareholders.

Inventory
Materials or products held by a company in the form of Raw Materials, Work in-Progress and Finished Goods.

Invoice
Document issued to a customer by a supplier as a request for payment in return for goods and services provided.

Key Performance Indicator (KPI)
An important measurement used to track a business's progress. KPIs are used to track trends in performance, to compare performance against benchmarks and to alert the business owner to potential opportunities and threat.

Liability
Debts (money, goods or services) that a person or business owes.

Liquid Asset
Assets which are either in the form of cash or can be turned into cash quickly.

Liquidity
The ability of a company to pay its short term liabilities.

Loan
Funding provided to a person or business, usually by a bank or finance company, with the expectation that it will be repaid at some time in the future. Interest payments are made or accrued in return for the loan..

Long Term Loan
A loan which is not due to be repaid within 12 months.

Long Term Liability
A liability which does not have to be repaid or settled within the next 12 months.

Mortgage
A loan for which the collateral is a specific asset - usually real estate.

Mortgage Repayment
A monthly payment to repay a mortgage.

Net
An amount that is left after other amounts have been deducted.

Net Assets (aka 'Net Worth')
The total assets of a company minus its liabilities.

Net Book Value
The value of an asset, as recorded in the company's accounts, after allowing for depreciation for wear and tear.

Net Income (aka 'Net Profit')
What remains after subtracting all the costs (including Cost of Goods Sold, rent, depreciation wages, interest, taxes etc.) from a company's total revenue. Net Income is sometimes referred to as"'the bottom-line.'.

Net Profit Margin
The ratio of Net Income to total sales revenue, expressed as a percentage.

Non-Current Asset
An asset used by a company on a long term or continuing basis.

Non-Current Liability
Any liability which will not be settled or paid within the next 12 months.

Non-Income Producing Asset
Any asset that is purchased by a company which will not generate a return or income for the business.

Non-Income Producing Expense
Any expenditure that is deducted by a company in computing Net Income but which was not necessary to the generation of that income e.g. purchasing flowers each week for the reception area).

Operating Expense
A fixed expense incurred by a company to generate income (but not including interest and tax).

Operating Expense Margin
Total Fixed Costs divided by total sales, expressed as a percentage.

Operating Profit
The profit from a business's main trading activity before taking into account interest and corporate tax.

Opportunity Cost
The cost of not using money, more productively and profitably than it is currently being used (or proposed to be used). Or, stated another way, the difference between the current return from a given investment and the potential return from better investment of the same money elsewhere.

Overdraft
A facility that lets a person access more money than they have in their account, for a charge.

Overheads
The Fixed costs of running a business, including rent, heat and light, advertising and salaries.

Paid-Up Share Capital
The money that shareholders have paid for the shares of a company.

Payable Days
The average number of days it takes for a company to pay its suppliers.

Profit (aka 'Net Profit')
The positive gain from an investment or business after subtracting all expenses Profit is the opposite of Loss and takes into account any accrued transactions (i.e. Accounts Payable and Accounts Receivable).

Profitability
The amount of profit made for each dollar invested in a company Usually measured by the Return On Assets or Return On Equity ratios.

Profit and Loss Statement - see *Income Statement.*

Receivable Days
The average number of days it takes a company to collect money owed to it.

Repayment
An amount currently due to be paid on money borrowed.

Retained Profits
Profits earned by a business that have not yet been spent (i.e. profite retained within the company).

Return
An amount, expressed as a percentage, that a person gets back when they invest or save money.

Return on Assets
Total Assets divided by Gross Profit.

Return on Equity
Net Profit divided by the owner's average Equity foe a given period.

Share Capital
Money invested directly in a company by its shareholders.

Security - see *Collateral.*

Share Price
The cost of buying a share on the stock market.

Secured Loan
A loan that is borrowed against a particular asset, known as collateral or security; if a person cannot make the repayments when they are due, the

lender can take ownership of the asset. A Mortgage is a particular type of Secured Loan

Shareholder
A person who owns a share or shares in a company.

Shareholder's' Equity (aka 'Owner's' Equity')
The portion of a company's assets that are owned by the Shareholders – share capital, share premium, retained profit and any other reserves. Should the company cease to operate, these would become owed to the Shareholders.

Tangible Assets
Assets that can be touched, such as equipment and furniture.

Term Loan
A loan that must be repaid within a certain period, for example four or five years.

Turnover (aka 'Sales' or 'Revenue')
The total value of a business' sales over a particular period.

Unsecured loan
A loan that is not backed by a particular asset; if a person does not pay back the loan, the lender cannot take any asset in lieu.

Variable Costs
Costs which are directly associated with the production of products or services and which rise or fall as production rises and falls. These might include. Cost of Goods Sold and the cost of subcontractors).

Variable Interest Rate
An interest rate on a loan that can be varied by the lending institution at any time.

Index

L

M

N

O

P

R

S

T

U

V

Made in United States
Troutdale, OR
11/03/2026

56844494R00116